Birds of South-eastern Australia
RARE

Susan McInnes commemorative edition

This book, the sixth in a series of seven books depicting the birds of south–eastern Australia, is dedicated to the memory of Susan McInnes, a gifted artist, who was the illustrator for this series and who died tragically with her husband Ivan in a natural disaster at Tamboon Inlet, East Gippsland in February 2002.

Susan was an all-round naturalist and a keen observer of wildlife, which is evidenced by the accurate and detailed colour plates as well as the wide range of small illustrations in each book.

The current revision of the series has been made possible by the expertise and commitment of Alan Reid, the generosity of Susan's sister, Jenny A Smith, and the goodwill of the Gould League.

Birds of South-eastern Australia
RARE

Illustrations by SUSAN McINNES
Revised by ALAN REID
Original text by ALAN REID, NOEL SHAW, ROY WHEELER

Birds of South-eastern Australia 6: Rare
ISBN 0 9578220 8 1

First published as *Birds of Victoria 6: Rare Species*
by the Gould League of Victoria, 1975
Reprinted 1979

This revised edition published by Overthefence Press, 2005
ABN: 37 586 900 504
75 Barreenong Road, Cottles Bridge Vic 3099
PO Box 6, Hurstbridge Vic 3099 Australia
T/ F: 61 (0)3 9714 8234
E: info@overthefencepress.com.au
W: www.overthefencepress.com.au

© Text Alan Reid, 2005, Illustrations estate of the late Susan McInnes, 2005
All rights reserved. No part of this publication may be produced in any form or by any means without the prior permission of the publishers.

Editorial and production by Tess Moloney
Text scanning by Maggie Lambert
Design by Green Poles Design
Layout by louladesign
Refereed by Sid Cowling, Birds Australia
Map prepared by Derrick Stone from data provided by Sid Cowling
Proofreading by Jenny A Smith and Felicity Nottingham
Pre-press by Book Repro and van Gastel Graphics
Printed in China by Everbest

National Library of Australia Cataloguing-in-Publication data

Reid, Alan.
Birds of South-eastern Australia.
Rev. ed.
ISBN 0 9578220 3 0 (1: Urban areas).
ISBN 0 9578220 4 9 (2: The ranges).
ISBN 0 9578220 5 7 (3: Oceans, bays and beaches).
ISBN 0 9578220 6 5 (4: Inland waters).
ISBN 0 9578220 7 3 (5: Dry country).
ISBN 0 9578220 8 1 (6: Rare).
ISBN 0 9578220 9 X (7: Farmlands).
ISBN 0 9752472 0 4 (1-7 set).

1. Birds - Australia. 2. Birds - Australia - Identification. 3. Birds - Australia - Geographical distribution. I. McInnes, Susan. II. Shaw, Noel. III. Wheeler, W. Roy (Wilson Roy). IV. Title.

598.0994

Front cover: Helmeted Honeyeater
Back cover: Channel-billed Cuckoo

Contents

How to use this book	vi
Introduction	1
Map of origins of some rare migratory and nomadic seabirds	2
Rare birds	3
Extinct species	7
Impact of global warming	9
Some rarer birds of south-eastern Australia	11
Birds of the ocean and beaches	14
Penguins 14, albatrosses, petrels, shearwaters 16,	
skuas, gulls, terns 26, waders, herons, hawks 32	
Birds of the southern plains and heaths	44
Parrots, quail 44, bristlebirds, finches 54	
Birds of the wetlands	58
Geese, ducks, reed birds	
Birds of the rainforests	64
Flycatchers, cockatoos, northern birds 64,	
honeyeaters, treecreepers 70	
Birds of the ranges	76
Honeyeaters, cuckoos, pigeons, owls	
Birds of the dry country	88
Parrots 88, honeyeaters, woodswallows, warblers 94,	
waders 106, hawks 108	
Birds of the northern plains	110
Bird list and index	112

How to use this book

Identifying a bird: Determine your habitat (the contents page might help) and go to the section of this book that is relevant; look up the bird's name in the index; or flip through and study the illustrations and descriptions.

Descriptions: These start with a bird's common name, scientific name, and size range. A bird's scientific name is in latin: the first part indicates its genus; the second its species; the third, where relevant, its sub-species. A bird's size is measured by the distance from the tip of its bill to the tip of its tail. (See *Birds 1: Urban Areas* p5 for size classes used.) Descriptions cover a bird's identifying features: what it looks like, how it sounds, how it flies, what it eats, what its nest looks like, how it behaves, and where it is found.

Illustrations: Birds of the same species can vary in colour and size because of their sex, age, sub-specific location, or even on an individual basis. The male and female of many species are similar. Where birds are markedly different, sex differences are indicated.

Similar species: This category indicates birds that are similar to the bird described. A similar species is not necessarily found in the same habitat.

Associated wildlife: Sketches of plants and animals that are present in a bird's habitat are provided with indicative measurements.

Cross-references: Page references to other books in this series are to fuller descriptions. (4:46), for example, refers to *Birds 4: Inland Waters*, page 46. An entire series index can be found in *Birds 1: Urban Areas*.

Abbreviations, symbols and terms: Standard abbreviations are used for measurements and geographical areas.

♀, ♂	female, male	NW	north-west(ern)
Aust	Australia(n)	NZ	New Zealand
C	celsius	p	page
cm	centimetre	Qld	Queensland
E	east, eastern	R	river, as in Murray R
eg	for example	S	south, southern
Great Divide	the Great Dividing Range	S Aust	southern Australia
ha	hectare	SA	South Australia
km	kilometre	SE	south-east(ern)
m	metre	Tas	Tasmania
mm	millimetre	Vic	Victoria
N	north, northern	W	west, western
NSW	New South Wales	WA	Western Australia

Introduction

This book covers the rare birds of south-eastern Australia. It was first published as *Birds of Victoria 6: Rare Species* in 1975 by the Gould League of Victoria, with the illustrations of Susan McInnes, who also illustrated the other revised guides in the series, and written by Alan Reid, Noel Shaw and Roy Wheeler.

There have been dramatic changes to the south-eastern region since 1975 and these include the setting aside of more parks and reserves, the impact of several severe drought periods, the widespread 1983 and 2002–03 bushfires, introduction of farm forestry practices on marginal lands, continued logging of old-growth forests, new controlled burning regimes by forest and park managers, fragmentation of larger bushland areas into vulnerable smaller 'island' remnants and the re-vegetation schemes and building of wildlife corridors by Land for Wildlife property owners and Landcare groups—each having some impact on the status of bird populations present.

The impact of global climate change should not be overlooked. Forecasts by ecologists such as Dr Harry Recher suggest that we may lose over half of our woodland bird species during the next 50 years if the current trends are maintained. Already there are concerns for species such as the Hooded Robin (p 102), Diamond Firetail (7:40), Grey-crowned Babbler (p 88) and Regent Honeyeater (p 76), once common on the mainland. On the beaches the Hooded Plover (p 38) is endangered, but conversely the Kelp Gull (p 26) has extended both its range and numbers and is now commonly seen along our southern coastline.

With massive changes in status, distribution and nomenclature of bird species across Australia over the past 30 years, it seems appropriate to reproduce the series with the original superb illustrations, but with text that reflects the current situation. So we have revised the book to include other birds now at risk.

Brolga 1050–1340 mm (4:32)

Origins of some rare migratory and nomadic seabirds

From tropical waters

Brown Booby; Leach's Storm-Petrel; Little and Wedge-tailed Shearwaters; frigatebirds; and tropicbirds

From Northern Hemisphere

Common, White-winged Black, Gull-billed and Arctic Terns; Long-tailed and Pomarine Jaegers; Whimbrel; sandpipers; knots; dotterels; and plovers

From New Zealand and Pacific Ocean

White-fronted Tern; Grey-backed Storm-Petrel; Mottled Petrel; Royal Albatross; and Erect-crested, Fiordland and Rockhopper Penguins

From Indian and Atlantic Oceans

Great-winged Petrel; Mottled Petrel; Yellow-nosed and Sooty Albatrosses; and Rockhopper Penguin

From Sub-Antarctic and Antarctic waters

Wilson's Storm-Petrel; Southern Fulmar, Blue and Kerguelen Petrels; Grey-headed Albatross; and King and Adelie Penguins

Rare birds

NOEL SHAW & ALAN REID

A Lyrebird (2:66) would be a rare sight indeed in Flinders Street, Melbourne, although it is far from rare in the undisturbed forests of south-eastern Australia. Even the Malleefowl (p111), a bird quite rightly described as rare, is not uncommon if you visit the few areas of mallee where it still lives. Some birds are rare no matter where you are, even it you are in an area where they like to live! Some parrots, owls, hawks and honeyeaters are examples of this type of rarity. In this book we have used three yardsticks to determine whether a species is rare.

We feel that a bird can be classed as rare in south-eastern Australia if:

(a) a species is not very numerous even though it has been recorded over a wide area of the state, for example, Black-eared Cuckoo (p110), Painted Snipe (p38), Osprey (p42), Sooty Owl (p82) and some seabirds and waders.

(b) a species, although not necessarily uncommon in some areas, is thought to represent a very small percentage of the total avian fauna in the region, for example, Helmeted Honeyeater (p76), Regent Honeyeater (p76), Turquoise Parrot (p90), and Ground Parrot (p44). Many of these species occupy a very restricted habitat that may be a remnant of a previously extensive area or are 'leftovers' from habitats that existed in previous geological periods. The rainforest pockets of East Gippsland in Victoria, for example, are all that remain of the rainforests that were widespread some million years ago, and the hillsides clothed with Blakely's Red Gum (*E blakelyi*) around Wangaratta contain a plant community that occurs more extensively on the central western slopes of NSW.

(c) a species, although perhaps more common in other regions, only occurs in south-eastern Australia on the extreme edge of its range, or occurs spasmodically in the region due to unusual climatic or other conditions that cause major disruption to its normal movements, for example, Chirruping Wedgebill (p104), Western Whipbird (p104), Inland Dotterel (p106), Australian Pratincole (p106), Brolga (4:32) and Black-faced Monarch (p64).

Inland Dotterel (p106)   Australian Pratincole (p106)

An extension of range can also occur because of the successful breeding of aviary escapees. Crested Pigeons (5:50) have colonised near the Melbourne Zoological Gardens, for example. Isolated colonies of Chestnut-breasted Mannikins and Scaly-breasted Lorikeets (p90) are also thought to be escapees, but could represent extensions of their natural range.

Because nature is not static, and while such diverse habitats are still available within the region, the picture of our bird populations will be constantly changing, as with recent sightings of the White-headed Pigeon and Emerald Dove (p86) in East Gippsland and the Channel-billed Cuckoo (p80) near Bendigo, Victoria. With the occurrence of sub-tropical rainforests in Eastern Gippsland, it is not unlikely that one day we may have further records of birds such as the Pheasant Coucal (p80), Rose-Crowned Fruit-Dove (p86) and Topknot Pigeon (p86) in the southern parts of the region.

Similarly the Plumed and Wandering Whistling-Ducks (p60) are occasionally sighted in south-eastern Australia and invasions of Freckled Ducks (p60) occur. Research may also reveal that some isolated populations of a species may be in fact a new species, as was discovered with the Forest Raven (2:88), Hall's Babbler and the Russet-tailed Thrush or that those which have been regarded as a separate species are now considered races of another species, such as the Yellow (5:70) and Adelaide (1:71) Rosellas and the Yellow-rumped Pardalote (5:52).

The status and range of other species is also changing—the Cattle Egret (4:50), Little Corella (p92) and Kelp Gull (p26) are prime examples of birds that have extended their range quite rapidly.

Another important influencing factor on our changing bird population is our own. The serious reduction—almost elimination in some cases—of areas of major habitats by clearing the plains, foothills and coastal heathlands for various forms of agriculture has resulted in a situation where very few sizeable examples of the original habitat can be found. Salination through over-clearing, accumulation of persistent pesticides and other residues, draining of wetlands and changes in environmental flow regimes have had

Freckled Duck (p60)

Wandering Whistling-Duck (p60)

similar impacts. It would be well nigh impossible to estimate the effect that this has had on many of our animals—we can only guess by reading the diaries of early settlers and explorers like Major Mitchell.

The introduction of a new species, both of birds and other animals, has also had effects on local bird numbers. Indian Mynas appear to have competed only too successfully for the dwindling number of hollow-tree nesting sites with some of the parrots and perhaps even kookaburras—and could eventually cause a decrease in local numbers for these species. The opposite also applies. Many of our species—Australian Magpies (2:52), Little Ravens (1:76), Masked Lapwings (4:14), Long–billed Corellas (p92), Noisy Miners (1:66), etc—have expanded their populations to fill the newly-created habitats caused by farming and forestry practices.

Victoria's seabirds and shoreline waders present a different picture. South-eastern Australia lies in the path of three major migration routes: the south-north winter movement of Antarctic dwellers, the north-south migration of the far-ranging northern hemisphere breeders, and the east-west, or west-east latitudinal movement of birds that breed in New Zealand or Indian Ocean waters. As well as the more common and regular visitors we are continually being visited by varying numbers of stragglers and vagrant species. The normal range of some is extended by chance or particular events and they find in Australian waters a place to rest before obeying their homing instincts to return to their breeding grounds. Many birds do not reach our shores alive but are washed up in varying states of decay. Others are so buffeted by storms that they are found bewildered and exhausted many miles from the sea, as would have been the Short-tailed Shearwater (3:16) found at Mildura and the Lesser Frigatebird (p24) found at Whitfield, to cite just two examples from inland Victoria.

The lists of recorded seabirds and waders will increase as more interested and informed observers add to our store of knowledge, either through their own expertise or by being aware of the need to send unfamiliar dead beach-washed specimens to their state museums for identification. Contact the nearest bird shelter to treat injured live birds. Most birds are, of course, already recorded but every now and then a new arrival is picked up, as was the case with the Arctic Tern (p30) specimen found inland at Camperdown in Victoria by David Morgan in 1953. This was followed by a beach-washed bird found by Alan Reid at Somers in 1960. From 1973 onwards, many more have been recorded along the Victorian coastline, perhaps indicating an expansion of range. The Black-winged Petrel is another example. The first pair was found alive by Alan Reid in a shearwater burrow on Heron Island in Queensland in 1962. Since then many have been recorded along the eastern coast and as far south as Tasmania.

With all species, but in particular the less common ones, the problem of protection is one of paramount importance. With migrant birds, both aquatic and terrestrial, whose breeding grounds (for example, Latham's Snipe 4:66) are elsewhere, we can do little but ensure that the adult birds are capable of making the return journey, and all that this implies. With our locally breeding species we must ensure that adequate areas of suitable habitat are maintained in a condition that will ensure that the species will be able to breed successfully. This raises the problem of rare and endangered species. Some species may be considered rare for one or other reason but may not necessarily be endangered—the Cape Barren Goose (p58), Malleefowl (p111) and Australian Bustard (p48), for instance. Other species are not only rare but are in danger of extinction, either through natural processes or through habitat modification by humans—as with the Regent Honeyeater (p76), Turquoise Parrot (p90), Forty-spotted Pardalote (p72), Superb Parrot (p88) and Orange-bellied Parrot (p46).

Regent Honeyeater (p76)

Superb Parrot (p88)

Over 900 bird species have now been recorded for the Australasian region. More than 60% of the locally breeding species are found nowhere else but in Australia, and many of these live precariously in some localised or special habitat. As well, some species that are common in other parts of Australia are rare, or only recorded occasionally in the south-east. Suitable habitats must be preserved to ensure that the widest possible diversity is maintained.

Extinct species

DOUG DORWARD

It has been said that extinction is a fact of life. Certainly there have been many more species in the past, than there are now and this is not because humans have extinguished them all. In the course of evolution, as circumstances and environments have changed in the world, some species have adapted and changed with them. Some have been unable to adapt and have died out.

We think of the disappearance of the Tasmanian Tiger, Paradise Parrot, King Island Emu, or indeed the Tasmanian Aborigine, as extinctions in recent or historical times and in some cases, associated with the impact of Europeans. The list of such species in Australia is not very long, however it is significant. But extinctions—and we know of only a small proportion of them from the fossil record—of the other sort, the more ancient type, are far more numerous and generally unremembered. For example, HT Condon (*Handlist of the Birds of South Australia*, South Australian Ornithological Association, Adelaide, 1969) listed 24 species of extinct birds, including a penguin, four kinds of flamingos, two pelicans, three storks, a swan, and five ducks. Of these, only one of the flamingos is recognisable as a modern species, and that of course is no longer found in this country.

Sir Richard Owen, the famous 19th century biologist, revealed that an extinct fauna of giant marsupials and reptiles, as well as birds, existed in inland South Australia some 70,000 years ago in the Pleistocene Period. These

Flamingos on the African salt lakes.

animals apparently lived in a habitat of saltbush and eucalyptus scrub indicating that at that time the rainfall was about twice what it is now. This shows us that even in this relatively short period of time quite remarkable changes in habitat have taken place, with consequent changes in bird populations and species, as well as other animals. It is this enormous geological time scale of hundreds of millions of years that we have to be clear about in trying to understand the difference between what we might call evolutionary extinction and human-induced extinction. The extinctions or population reductions produced by humans in the last few hundred years (and those that we seem likely to produce in the next few decades) have taken place at relatively great speeds compared with the earlier ones, and furthermore if viewed in the relative time scale are almost certainly far more numerous, per unit of time.

Once we understand this, then, we can be realistic about the present situation. Our concern is not merely the preservation of species, because many have come and gone in the past, but about the present very rapid rate of change in fortune among other species caused primarily by one of them, homo sapiens.

One thing we do is artificially increase the distribution of species that could not spread by themselves, and so we have sparrows, starlings, mynas, and turtle-doves where perhaps we think they should not be.

The Cape Barren Goose (p58) is another case in point; it is probably now as common as it has ever been, at least in some places. Before pastures were developed it depended during summer on native vegetation such as adjacent to lakes in Victoria's Western District. On the Furneaux Group islands in Bass Strait and along the South Gippsland coast, pasture improvement has gone so far that the geese are easily able to survive summer shortages of food on their breeding islands by flying to farmland, and are now so numerous that they have become a considerable nuisance to farmers. Nevertheless, as a species the Cape Barren Goose is still of very local occurrence and in world terms is one of the rarest of waterfowl. The Helmeted Honeyeater (p76) survives in small numbers not far from the eastern outskirts of Melbourne. As the city spread eastwards, the once peripheral market gardens and orchards were swallowed up by suburbia and the gardeners and farmers moved a step further out. So even the Helmeted Honeyeaters' reserve at Yellingbo is becoming swamped by the expanding city and urban services, and its habitat, fast becoming an island, will not be sufficient for its survival.

Impact of global warming — ALAN REID

During our planet's history there have been many rapid warmings and coolings of the earth and its atmospheric envelope with rapid advances and retreats of the icecaps. Each episode has led to mass extinctions and shifts of wildlife populations. The past 80 years have seen the beginning of yet another global warming period and coupled with extensive modification of the landscape and waterways, habitat fragmentation and the introduction of exotic animals, more massive changes to wildlife populations are predicted.

The average world temperature rose by 0.7°C between 1910 and 1990. Many experts believe this process is accelerating. CSIRO expects temperatures in Australia to rise 0.4 to 2°C by the year 2030 and 1 to 6°C by 2070 when atmospheric greenhouse gas concentrations will be double pre-industrial levels. Between 1990 and 2000 Australia has experienced 9 of the 10 warmest years on record.

If a mid-range 3°C rise occurs, this will equate to a 300km latitude shift southwards and a 500m increase in elevation, and it is estimated that up to 90 Australian animal species and several eucalypt species will then be at risk. The Snow Gum *Eucalyptus pauciflora* will have to migrate 400 times faster than its known upslope migration rate to keep up with the shifting climate zones. Warming will be greatest in spring and least in winter, and most locations in south-eastern Australia will have less rainfall at these times. Sea levels will rise by 9 to 88cm by the year 2100 under the 1 to 6°C scenario.

Around Heard Island in the Antarctic, sea levels are rising, sea surface temperatures have risen up to 1°C since 1947 and 12% of glacial cover has been lost. Right across the world, glaciers are retreating. Norway, Canada and the Andean countries of South America have all recorded rapid retreats over the past few years.

Ecologist Dr Harry Recher points out that without action to restore functional ecosystems and feral animal control, Australia is likely to lose more than half of its terrestrial bird species during this century. There is already a decline in ground-dwelling treecreepers and woodland ground-feeding birds, such as the Speckled Warbler (p102), Buff-rumped Thornbill (7:72), Hooded Robin (p102) and Southern Whiteface (5:20), which are fast disappearing from woodland remnants.

There is also a threat to the birds of the canopy. Global warming is leading to earlier budding, flowering and fruiting of many plant species around the world. It is also influencing migration and movement patterns of birds and mammals and the emergence times of insects. Migrating flycatchers and honeyeaters, which have always relied on arthropod or nectar abundance for feeding their newly hatched young, may soon find food supplies diminishing at critical nesting times during late spring and early summer. Long-term flowering studies have shown that many Australian plants are now flowering more than four weeks earlier than they did 20 years ago.

Bird observers, by keeping records of first flowering, arrival dates of migrating birds, successful bird nesting and insect emergence times, can make a real contribution to our understanding of the rate of change and the nature of the impact of global warming on our native bird populations.

They should contact the Biowatch program at Macquarie University and contribute to the website at <www.bio.mq.ed.au/ecology/biowatch/Biowatch.htm>.

Buff-rumped Thornbill 100–110mm (7:72)   Southern Whiteface 100–125mm (5:20)

The format (7:72) refers to the book and page number in this series where a full description of the species can be found.

Some rarer birds of south-eastern Australia — ROY WHEELER

From the writings of our early settlers like Batman, Howitt, Backhouse, Wheelwright, Batey, AJ Campbell, Keartland and others, we have a very good picture of the abundance of bird species. Even in those times, in many cases over a century ago, they gave warnings that some species were disappearing fast. In south-eastern Australia this impact has been felt among several species, although the few that are now rare or extinct within the region are still in good numbers elsewhere in Australia.

Since Europeans came to Australia, it appears that only one species has become officially extinct. It is the Paradise Parrot of Central Qeensland and northern New South Wales. The Night Parrot was earlier classified as extinct, but in 1990 a fresh corpse was found in the Mt Isa Uplands.

Among breeding species lost to south-eastern Australia are the Magpie Goose (p58) and the Australian Bustard (p48). In the early days of settlement, most pioneers lived off the land and these birds, being large and good game, were extensively hunted. Large numbers still existed until the 1880s and then gradually they became rare, and since that time occasional birds have visited the region but no breeding has taken place, except at Serendip, near Lara in Victoria where conservation authorities have been endeavouring to re-establish them.

Many of our species classified as rare have always been rare, even before European settlement: birds like the three less common owls (Sooty, Masked and Powerful, p82), and others like the Scarlet-chested Parrot (p90), Chirruping Wedgebill (p104), Black-eared Miner (p111), Inland Thornbill (5:18), White Goshawk (p42) and Spotted Bowerbird (p98), all of which breed in south-eastern Australia. Other rare birds are regular visitors such as the Orange-bellied Parrot (p46), and unless their breeding areas are protected, all we can hope is that they get full protection during their stay on the mainland.

Some birds whose habitats now need special protection are the Helmeted Honeyeater (p76), Ground Parrot (p44), Turquoise Parrot (p90), Malleefowl (p111), Southern Emu-wren (7:70), Eastern Bristlebird (p54), Grey-crowned Babbler (p88), Plains-wanderer (p52), Regent Honeyeater (p76), Bush Stone-curlew (p38) and Orange-bellied Parrot (p46).

The Helmeted Honeyeater (p76) is now considered a sub-species of the Yellow-tufted Honeyeater (2:30), but it is just as important to attempt conservation of the rarer races and sub-species of even the most common birds. Although not threatened at this stage, the various races of the Australian Ringneck (5:60), Crimson Rosella (2:42), Varied Sittella (2:36) and Spotted Pardalote (5:52) fit this category.

The Ground Parrot (p44) lives in damp coastal heaths and once occurred practically along the entire south-eastern coast. It still occurs in small numbers, in the heaths around Portland and Wilsons Promontory National Park, inland at Chapple Vale in the western Otways and in the heathlands between Green Cape in New South Wales and Marlo in eastern Victoria. It is still moderately common in western Tasmania. Recently-declared coastal national parks, should help preserve this rare bird on the mainland.

The Eastern Bristlebird (p54) is confined to the tea-tree thickets of coastal south-eastern Australia from Barren Grounds in New South Wales to Marlo in Victoria and, like the Ground Parrot, is afforded protection by Croajingalong National Park.

Diamond Firetail 120–130mm (7:40)

White-browed Babbler 180–220mm (5:48)

Bush Stone-curlew 550–590mm (5:22)

Southern Emu-wren 150–190mm (7:70)

The Malleefowl (p111) is regarded as rare in Western Australia, South Australia and New South Wales and endangered in Victoria. All these states are endeavouring to keep this interesting bird by establishing national parks and fauna reserves but time is against us.

The gradual disappearance of the Grey-crowned Babbler (p88), White-browed Babbler (5:48), Diamond Firetail (7:40) and Bush Stone-curlew (5:22) from areas in central and western Victoria is causing concern. Foxes, feral cats, illicit shooters and loss of habitat have contributed to their declining numbers. All occurred in numbers near Melbourne and other areas in western Victoria 75 years ago, but now have nearly disappeared. They still occur in numbers in New South Wales and Queensland and it is to be hoped that by establishing national parks, forest reserves and fauna reserves where these birds still survive, that they will be saved the fate of the Magpie Goose (p58) and the Australian Bustard (p48).

Finally the story of the Turquoise Parrot (p90) is well worth repeating. This small beautifully-coloured parrot became extinct within Victoria about 80 years ago. Loss of habitat, bird trappers and competition for nesting hollows with introduced species no doubt all had a great deal to do with their decline, not only in Victoria but in New South Wales as well. A few years ago it filtered into north-eastern Victoria and occurs now in small numbers with occasional sightings further south. It appears to have also recovered in New South Wales. Conservation and the preservation of our rare breeding species should be the aim of us all. It is only by constant watching and positive action that these birds can be retained for generations to come.

RARER SEABIRDS AND WADERS

Every year brings new records as keen observers take a closer look at the mixed flocks of seabirds and waders that patrol our coastlines. Some of these may be stragglers caught up by a flock of a different species. Others, especially birds from southern latitudes, are driven out of their normal ranges. Many arrive in very poor condition, and some are beach-washed. Any dead 'stranger' should be sent to your local museum for identification. A few waders, especially younger ones, stay and may be seen sheltering on rocky spits during winter storms, although most leave in early autumn for the long flight back to the breeding grounds.

Cooperative wader banding schemes in Australia, SE Asia and Russia have done much to uncover migratory paths and important feeding and breeding grounds.

Birds of the ocean and beaches

PENGUINS

Large flightless seabirds mostly confined to cooler waters of southern hemisphere. Food (crabs, squid and fish) is caught under water. Nest in colonies, 1–2 eggs laid in burrow, on ground or ice. Adult crested penguins have conspicuous crests above eyes and a thick bill.

① **ERECT-CRESTED PENGUIN** *Eudyptes sclateri* 670–710 mm
General: Large, massive red bill surrounded by white skin. Bright yellow to orange crest turns upward above crown. **Nest:** Breeds sub-Antarctic region south of NZ. **Distribution:** Records from Vic, SA and Tas.

② **FIORDLAND PENGUIN** *Eudyptes pachyrhynchus* 550–650 mm
General: Large-sized crested penguin with white cheek striations. No white skin edging to red beak. **Nest:** Breeds S NZ islands. **Distribution:** Regular winter-spring visitor to SE Aust, mostly immature.

③ **KING PENGUIN** *Aptenodytes patagonicus* 850–950 mm
General: Large, silver-grey, glossy black head, orange ear-patch and bib, long black bill with pinkish base, white breast. Powerful swimmer, dolphin-like. **Nest:** Breeds sub-Antarctic islands, egg incubated in skin fold above feet. **Distribution:** S Atlantic and S Indian Oceans, vagrant to Tas, Vic, WA.

④ **ADELIE PENGUIN** *Pygoscelis adeliae* 700–760 mm
General: Large, brown-black head, throat and back, white breast, white eye-ring, short brown bill. Immature white throat, black eye-ring. **Nest:** Breeds Antarctic coast. **Distribution:** Heard and Macqarie Islands. Some Tas.

⑤ **ROCKHOPPER PENGUIN** *Eudyptes chrysocome* 450–610 mm
General: Large penguin. Black head and back, black and yellow crest, reddish bill. Immature duller, lacks yellow plumes. **Nest:** Breeds sub-Antarctic islands. **Distribution:** Western form *mosleyi* occurs frequently during winter, moulting immature seen in summer in SE Aust. Differs from rare eastern form *filholi* with no pale pink skin edging beak and by flipper pattern.

SIMILAR SPECIES FROM REGION

Macaroni (Royal) Penguin
650–750 mm

Chinstrap Penguin
700–760 mm

Snares Penguin
510–610 mm

ALBATROSSES

Very large seabirds with wide wing-span, enabling them to soar and glide expertly. Heavy beak has nostril 'tubes' at sides. Food is pelagic: squid, fish, etc, and refuse. Most species breed on sub-Antarctic islands in summer and disperse during winter when many appear around southern coasts. Shy Albatross breeds on 3 islands around Tas and on sub-Antarctic islands.

⑥ **ROYAL ALBATROSS** *Diomedea epomophora* 1070–1270 mm
General: Very large. Similar to Wandering Albatross (3:12). Pure white head and body, mostly black upperwings, large pale bill. 2 distinct forms. **Nest:** Smaller *D e sanfordi* breeds NZ on South Island and Chatham Island; larger *D e epomophora* breeds S NZ. **Distribution:** *D e sanfordi* visits SE Aust. May–Sept; *D e epomophora* moderately common all months.

⑦ **YELLOW-NOSED ALBATROSS** *Diomedea chlororhynchos* 710–820 mm
General: Large, white body, black upperwings. Slender black bill has yellow top. **Nest:** Breeds N sub-Antarctic islands of Atlantic and Indian Oceans. **Distribution:** Becoming frequent visitor along S coast. May–Oct. Race *bassi* most commonly seen.

⑧ **GREY-HEADED ALBATROSS** *Diomedea chrysostoma* 700–850 mm
General: Large, white, grey head, black upperwings. Black bill with yellow above and below. Immature browner, black bill, black and dark-grey underwing with white 'window'. **Nest:** Breeds circumpolar sub-Antarctic islands. **Distribution:** Regular but uncommon migrant to SE Aust waters. May–Nov.

⑨ **LIGHT-MANTLED SOOTY ALBATROSS** *Phoebetria palpebrata* 780–900 mm
General: Slender, large, grey. Darker head, wings and rump; incomplete white eye-ring. **Nest:** Breeds sub-Antarctic islands. **Distribution:** Rare visitor to SE Aust waters. May–Oct.

⑩ **SOOTY ALBATROSS** *Phoebetria fusca* 840–890 mm
General: Slender, large, dark grey to sooty brown, yellow stripe on each side on dark bill, incomplete white eye-ring. **Nest:** Breeds on sub-Antarctic islands in S Atlantic and S Indian Oceans. **Distribution:** Rare but regular visitor to S Aust waters.

SIMILAR SPECIES

Southern Giant-Petrel 850–1000mm (3:14)

Northern Giant-Petrel 800–950mm (3:14)

PETRELS

Seabirds with tube-shaped nostrils, only coming on land to breed. Food is small surface-dwelling ocean creatures, skimmed from surface, while in flight or sitting on water, also refuse and carrion.

GADFLY PETRELS

Petrels with stout bills and long wings, sweeping flight interspersed with glides.

(11) **GREAT-WINGED PETREL** *Pterodroma macroptera* 380–430 mm
General: Medium-large, dark brown, pale around bill, paler brown along underwing margins. **Nest:** Breeds WA, NZ and sub-Antarctic islands. 1 white egg in burrow. May–Nov. **Distribution:** Moderately common most SE Aust waters during winter.

(12) **MOTTLED PETREL** *Pterodroma inexpectata* 330–350 mm
General: Medium-large, thickset. Scaly grey and 'M' pattern on upper-wings; white throat, grey belly. Black bill, legs flesh-pink. **Nest:** breeds S NZ islands. **Distribution:** Very rare straggler to SE Aust. Sept–Jan.

(13) **SOFT-PLUMAGED PETREL** *Pteodroma mollis* 320–370 mm
General: Dark blue-grey above, grey chest-band across white underparts. White forehead mottled black, broad black eye mark. Dark 'M' wing-band above and below. **Nest:** Breeds sub-Antarctic islands, also south of NZ. **Distribution:** Moderately common visitor to S Aust waters, mostly May–Oct.

(14) **KERGUELEN PETREL** *Lugensa brevirostris* 330–360 mm
General: Similar to but smaller than Great-winged. Grey-brown body and wings. **Nest:** Breeds sub-Antarctic islands in S Atlantic and S Indian Oceans. **Distribution:** Rare straggler to S Aust waters. Jun–Oct.

(15) **GOULD'S PETREL** *Pterodroma leucoptera* 300–310 mm
General: Medium-sized blue-grey petrel with dark crown and M band. Underwings white with narrow black edges, white below, darker tail. Quick wing-beats and glides. **Nest:** Breeds Cabbage tree Island off NSW coast. 1 white egg on ground. Oct–May. **Distribution:** Disperses through Tasman Sea. Some beachwashed in SE Aust.

(16) **BLUE PETREL** *Halobaena caerulea* 260–320 mm
General: Medium-sized blue petrel, dark crown, black 'M' band, white-tipped tail, white below. Legs blue, pink webs. **Nest:** Large colonies on sub-Antarctic islands. **Distribution:** Rather rare straggler with other petrels to S Aust waters. May–Sept.

SHEARWATERS AND LARGE PETRELS

Dark gregarious petrels with narrow wings held rigid while gliding low over water. Rapid shallow wing-beats often touching surface. Pelagic food scooped up while bird diving or swimming. They nest in long burrows.

⑰ **LITTLE SHEARWATER** *Puffinus assimilis* 250–300mm
General: Medium-sized, blue-black above, white below. Flies fast, low, direct with rapid wing-beats and glides. **Nest:** 1 white egg in burrow on islands off WA, Lord Howe Island, Norfolk Island, NZ, S Atlantic and Indian Oceans. **Distribution:** Rather rare visitor to SE Aust waters. Sept–Mar.

⑱ **HUTTON'S SHEARWATER** *Puffinus huttoni* 360–380mm
General: Similar to, slightly larger and darker than Fluttering Shearwater (3:16), grey and white underparts, white abdomen. **Nest:** Breeds South Island, NZ. Sept–Apr. **Distribution:** Rather rare, but off-shore SE Aust most months.

⑲ **WEDGE-TAILED SHEARWATER** *Puffinus pacificus* 380–460mm
General: Medium-large, dark, grey-black bill, broad wings, long wedged tail; some pale beneath. **Nest:** Breeds islands off E and W Aust coast. 1 white egg. Oct–May. **Distribution:** Moderately common NSW coast, vagrant S coasts.

⑳ **FLESH-FOOTED SHEARWATER** *Puffinus carneipes* 400–450mm
General: Medium-large, brown-black, pale black-tipped bill, pinkish feet, short squarish tail. Slow shallow wing-beats and glides. **Nest:** Breeds Lord Howe Island, NZ, WA coast and islands. **Distribution:** Moderately common NSW coast, rare Vic, Tas.

㉑ **SOOTY SHEARWATER** *Puffinus griseus* 400–460mm
General: Larger, slimmer, longer-billed than Short-tailed (3:16). Dark brown above, pale wing-stripe below. **Nest:** 1 white egg Sept–Apr. Breeds NZ and islands south, NSW, Tas and off-shore islands. **Distribution:** Rather rare SE Aust waters. Oct–Feb.

㉒ **WHITE-CHINNED PETREL** *Procellaria aequinoctialis* 510–580mm
General: Large, brown-black, strong pale bill, white chin-patch, black feet. Follows ships, flying low. **Nest:** Breeds sub-Antarctic islands. **Distribution:** Moderately common SE Aust coast. Mar–Jul.

㉓ **GREY PETREL** *Procellaria cinerea* 450–510mm
General: Medium-large, slender-winged, ash-grey above, white below. Dark brown on head, wings and tail, bill greenish with black ridge, feet pale, dives from height. **Nest:** Breeds sub-Antarctic islands, NZ region. **Distribution:** Rather rare visitor to SE Aust waters most months.

STORM-PETRELS

Small, usually dark, 'wave-hopping' seabirds with short, hooked bills. Flight rapid, erratic with feet dangling; pelagic, food collected in flight. Single egg laid in long burrows on cool temperate islands of both hemispheres. Extensive migration during non-breeding months.

(24) LEACH'S STORM-PETREL *Oceanodroma leucorhoa* 190–250mm
General: Medium-sized, like Wilson's but paler, slimmer, longer forked tail. Flight butterfly-like. **Nest:** Breeds N Atlantic and Pacific coasts. **Distribution:** Rare vagrant on S Aust coast.

(25) GREY-BACKED STORM-PETREL *Garrodia nereis* 160–190mm
General: Medium-small, grey-brown head and upper body, white underparts, black edges to wings. Bat-like fluttering over waves. **Nest:** Breeds NZ region, Macquarie Island. **Distribution:** Regular but rarely-sighted winter visitor.

(26) WILSON'S STORM-PETREL *Oceanites oceanicus* 150–190mm
General: Medium-small, sooty-brown, white rump, short rounded wing, dances across surface, feet dragging when feeding. **Nest:** Breeds Antarctica, Nov-May. **Distribution:** Moderately common off-shore SE Aust. May-Jun.

(27) SOUTHERN (Antarctic) FULMAR *Fulmarus glacialoides* 450-500mm
General: Medium-large, blue-grey, gull-like, paler head, underparts. Darker wings. Bill pink, black-tipped. **Distribution:** Breeds Antarctica, irregular visitor S waters. Jun-Jan.

PRIONS

Small, short-winged petrels with black tail tip. Flight fast, erratic with sideways twists, exposing lighter underbody and dove-grey upperparts alternately. M-shaped mark on upperwings. Food includes krill, often seen in company with whales feeding on krill. Most common prion in SE Aust is Fairy Prion 230–280mm (3:18). Others less common include Salvin's Prion 250–300mm, Slender-billed Prion 250–260mm, Broad-billed Prion 280–320mm and Fulmar Prion 270–290mm. A look-alike is the darker, short-billed Common Diving-Petrel 200–250mm (3:18).

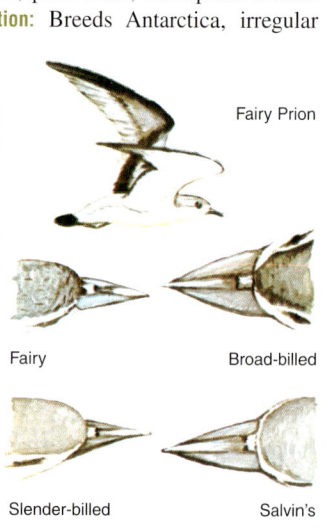

Fairy Prion

Fairy

Broad-billed

Slender-billed

Salvin's

WEB-FOOTED SEABIRDS

Large ocean-going birds, with long wings, short legs and all toes connected by webbing. All adept at soaring and dive from considerable heights into sea after fish. Frigatebirds 'pirate' the food of other seabirds as well as scavenge. Nest on rocky islands, cliffs, trees, bushes, or use scrape in ground, sometimes lined with sticks, etc. One egg laid (2 in case of Brown Booby). Generally colonial nesters. Very rare Cape Gannet of South Africa is vagrant, seen at Portland and interbreeding with Australasian Gannet on Wedge Light in Port Phillip Bay, Vic.

(28) RED-TAILED TROPICBIRD *Phaethon rubricauda* 610–860 mm
General: Large white bird with pink shades on wings and back. 2 long red feathers with black centres extend beyond tail (up to 300mm). Birds feed well out to sea, diving from considerable heights for fish. **Nest:** Breeds on tropical islands, 1 pale egg spotted red-brown. **Distribution:** Rare stragglers are collected and sighted in S waters. Occasional storm-driven birds occur well inland.

(29) LESSER FRIGATEBIRD *Fregata ariel* 700–800 mm
General: Large black seabird with deeply forked tail. Male has white patches on body under the wing and bright red or orange distensible pouch under chin. Larger female has white abdomen. **Nest:** Breeds on tropical islands in Aust and elsewhere. 1 white egg, flat stick nest. **Distribution:** Common in north, very rare straggler in south.

(30) GREAT FRIGATEBIRD *Fregata minor* 850–1050 mm
General: Larger than preceding species. Adult male is all black with exception of red, distensible, gular pouch. Larger female resembles that of Lesser Frigatebird but has grey under neck. **Nest:** Breeds on islands in Coral Sea and other tropical oceans. Stick platform, 1 white egg. **Distribution:** Not as common as previous species in N Aust. Very rare in S waters.

(31) BROWN BOOBY *Sula leucogaster* 650–750 mm
General: Large brown seabirds with white abdomen and central underwing. Facial skin and base of greyish bill is blue in male and yellow in female. **Nest:** Breeds on sub-tropical and tropical islands in Aust and elsewhere. 2 pale green eggs. Fishes in shallower water than other gannets. **Distribution:** Common in northern waters, rare to very rare straggler in S areas. Few S records.

SKUAS AND GULLS

Gregarious web-footed birds, scavenging or pelagic in food gathering, often 'pirating' other birds' food. Preys on eggs and chicks of other species. Flight rapid and acrobatic. Darker skuas distinguished from immature larger gulls by white underwing flashes, hawk-like flight. Central tail-feathers project in the 3 jaegers. Usually 2 eggs laid in scrape or depression on coastal islands.

32 ARCTIC JAEGER *Stercorarius parasiticus* 410–460mm
General: Medium-large, dark brown, yellow neck and side of head, dark cap. Light phase has white underparts, pale wing flashes. Straight, pointed, projecting tail-feathers. **Distribution:** Moderately common visitor from Arctic region.

33 GREAT SKUA *Catharacta skua* 610–660mm
General: Large, brown, streaked darker brown. Broad pale wing-stripe, bill and feet pink. **Distribution:** Breeds Antarctic and sub-Antarctic islands. Rather rare visitor to S Aust coastal waters, May-Sept.

34 POMARINE JAEGER *Stercorarius pomarinus* 460–520mm
General: Medium-large; elongated, blunt, twisted central tail-feathers. Light and dark phases, the latter totally dark brown, well-defined white wing-bars, the former with light collar and underwing, white underparts, dark chest-band. Immature barred brown. **Distribution:** Breeds Arctic, migrates to Aust and other S waters Nov-Feb. Often sighted Vic, rarer Tas, SA.

35 LONG-TAILED JAEGER *Stercorarius longicaudus* 500-550mm
General: Large, dark, summer visitors from Arctic with 2 central tail-feathers greatly elongated. 2 phases—very rare all dark brown form and more common light form, grey-brown above, dark cap, white collar, whitish underparts. **Distribution:** Regular migrants but sightings rare.

36 KELP GULL *Larus dominicanus* 550–600mm
General: Large, pure white tail, greenish-yellow legs, red spot on lower mandible. Immature mottled brown, bill black. **Distribution:** Breeds NZ, sub-Antarctic islands and around S Aust coastline. Rather rare, moderately common in S Tas.

37 PACIFIC GULL *Larus pacificus* 580–660mm
General: Larger, more common than Kelp Gull. Red spot on both mandibles. Black sub-terminal band on tail, yellowish legs. **Distribution:** Breeds off-shore islands along S Aust coast. Sedentary, common.

Other rare visitors include Franklin's Gull and the South Polar Skua.

LOCAL TERNS

Slightly built, short legs, forked tails. Most grey and white with blackish heads, sometimes with crest, some dusky in colour. Food caught while diving or scooped from surface. Breeding and eclipse plumages usually differ.

(38) LITTLE TERN *Sterna albifrons* 210–240 mm
General: Medium-sized, pearl-grey above, white forehead and underparts. Crown, nape, line between beak and eye black. Bill yellow with black tip, legs orange-yellow. Immature darker. Both immature and non-breeding adults have crown streaked with white, lack stripe from bill to eye. **Voice:** Soft, high-pitched 'kree-k'. **Flight:** Very swift, buoyant and erratic. Low over water. **Nest:** Depression in sand just above high tide mark. 2–3 cream or stone-colored eggs, blotched and spotted grey and brown. Nov–Feb. **Behaviour:** In flocks during summer months. Catches fish by diving. **Distribution:** Rather rare in south, more common in north, along SE Aust coast. Endangered, number of colonies reducing rapidly. Beach nests subject to disturbance by humans and domestic pets.

(39) FAIRY TERN *Sterna nereis* 210–250 mm
General: Pearl-grey above, white forehead and underparts. Bill and feet orange-yellow. Immature dark beaks. **Voice:** Similar to Little Tern. **Flight:** Rapid, buoyant with zig-zag movements. **Nest:** In colonies on sand among shell fragments and beach flotsam. 2 yellowish-grey eggs blotched brown and grey. Breeds on quiet beaches, islands and sand-spits Oct–Jan. **Behaviour:** In small or large groups. Follows intruders, scolding and wheeling. Often roosts on sandbars with other seabirds. Dives for prey after hovering. **Distribution:** Rather rare in NSW, Vic and Tas; still common in WA and SA.

(40) ROSEATE TERN *Sterna dougallii* 350–380 mm
General: Graceful, medium-large, black cap, long white tail-feathers and underparts suffused delicate pink. Breeding adults: red bill, legs; non-breeding: white forehead, dark bill. **Behaviour:** Buoyant flight, shallow wing-beats. Sand-scrape nest 1–2 grey, brown-spotted eggs; summer or autumn nesting, varying with location.
Distribution: Breeding resident of WA and Qld reefs and coastal islands. Few records south of Ballina, NSW unconfirmed.

breeding (40)

OCEAN AND BEACHES

MIGRATORY TERNS

Migrants often obtain full or partial breeding plumage before departure.

(41) WHITE-WINGED BLACK TERN *Chlidonias leucopterus* 220–240 mm
General: Usually seen in grey and white non-breeding plumage in summer, some attaining red legs, black body and underwing before departure. Smaller than similar Whiskered Tern (4:80). **Distribution:** Migrant from Eurasia. Sept–May. Rather rare in south, more common in north.

(42) COMMON TERN *Sterna hirundo* 320–380 mm
General: Similar to Arctic Tern but with white underparts, black cap, red bill with black tip in breeding plumage. Non-breeding bird has extensive white forehead and tail, black bill. Immature mottled above. **Distribution:** N hemisphere breeder. Moderately common summer visitor to SE Aust; some immature birds over-winter.

(43) GULL-BILLED TERN *Sterna nilotica* 370–430 mm
General: Breeding plumage similar to Crested Tern, massive back bill and less forked tail; black on head restricted to eye region in non-breeding birds. **Nest:** 2 pale eggs, blotched red. Inland lake islands. Sept–May. **Distribution:** Disperses from inland nesting sites. Rather rare in south, more common in north.

(44) ARCTIC TERN *Sterna paradisaea* 330–380 mm
General: Light grey, deeply forked tail. Breeding birds black heads, white rump, red bill and legs. Non-breeding in Aust. Bill and legs black, forehead and tail white. **Distribution:** Breeds far north. Rather rare all months S Aust.

(45) WHITE-FRONTED TERN *Sterna striata* 360–420 mm
General: Eclipse plumage—like Common Tern, tail less forked, black leading and white trailing edges to wings, dark in front of eye. Breeding plumage—black cap extends to front of eye, white underparts rosy. **Nest:** 2 grey eggs, blotched black. Oct–Dec. **Distribution:** Rather rare to moderately common SE Aust coast. Migrant from NZ but small breeding colonies now established on Furneaux Group islands, Tas.

(46) ANTARCTIC TERN *Sterna vittata* 400–420 mm
General: Heavier, longer bill than Arctic Tern. Undulating flights, almost vertical diving for food. Shrill, high-pitched call. Bill and legs redden, plumage turns blue-grey during breeding period. Oct–Apr. **Distribution:** Rare migrant from Antarctica to WA, SA and Vic waters.

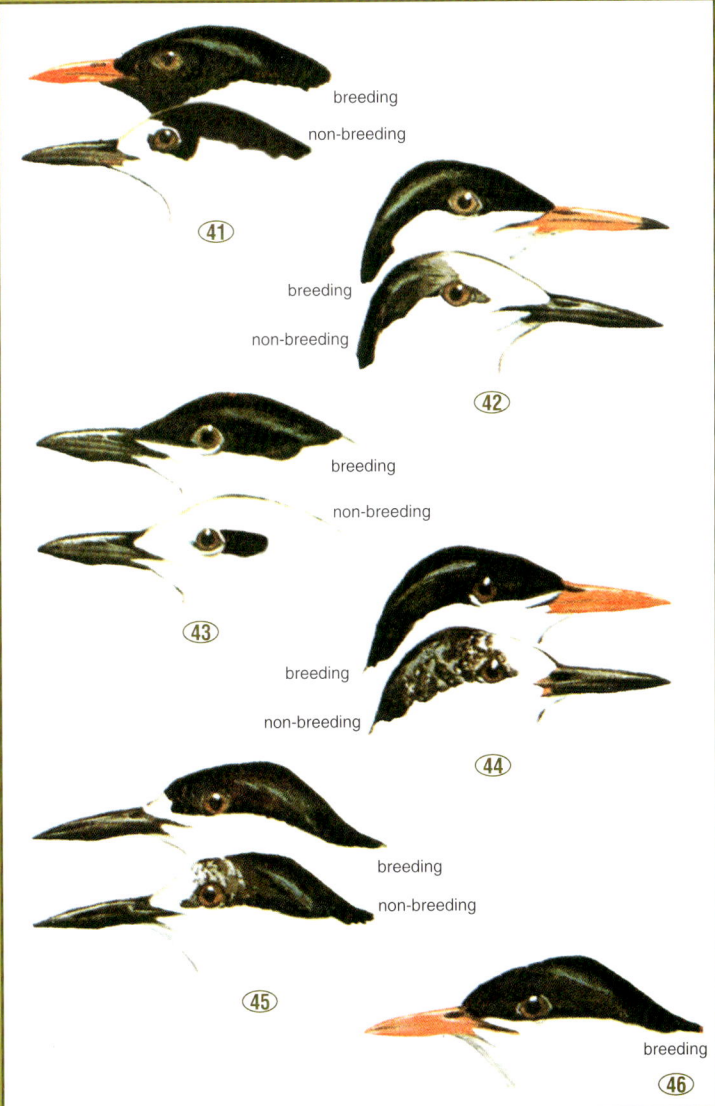

RARER MIGRATORY WADERS

Shorebirds gather in large restless mixed species flocks before leaving Aust in March and April for their northern hemisphere breeding grounds. They can be heard returning in their thousands on moonlit nights in Aug and Sept. These rarer species will be among them.

㊼ **LONG-TOED STINT** *Calidris subminuta* 130–160 mm

General: Small, short, rounded sandpiper with small head, short straight bill and long neck. Associates with other small waders, feeding in shallows. Flies high, calling loudly, when flushed. **Distribution:** Uncommon but regular visitor to SE. Breeds in E Siberia.

㊽ **ORIENTAL PLOVER** *Charadrius veredus* 220–250 mm

General: Slender upright plover, long legs and wings, distinctive buff collar above white breast. Strong erratic flight; 'chip-chip-chip', trilling and piping calls. Associates with pratincoles and Inland Dotterel. Breeds Mongolia, E China. **Distribution:** Rather rare but regular migrant to SE Aust. Sept–Mar.

㊾ **DUNLIN** *Calidris alpina* 160–220mm

General: Medium-small hunched brown and white wader with short neck, wings and legs and slightly decurved bill near tip. Only one authenticated record, near Cairns. (Several unconfirmed in SE.) **Distribution:** Breeds in N Eurasia and N America.

㊿ **GREATER SAND PLOVER** *Charadrius leschenaultii* 220–250 mm

General: Heavy-billed, long-legged, brown and white plover in mixed flocks with other waders, running in typical stop/start fashion. Call a rattling trill. Breeds S Siberia, Afghanistan. **Distribution:** Rather rare S coast, Aug–May.

(51) **LESSER SAND PLOVER** *Charadrius mongolus* 190–210 mm

General: Similar but smaller than Greater Sand Plover, more upright, smaller more slender bill, smaller head. Often associated with Double-banded Plover (3:48). Call a soft trill. Breeds in Mongolia. **Distribution:** Rather rare S coast, Aug–May.

STAGES IN DEVELOPMENT OF A TYPICAL WADER
Red-capped Plover 140–160 mm (3:48)

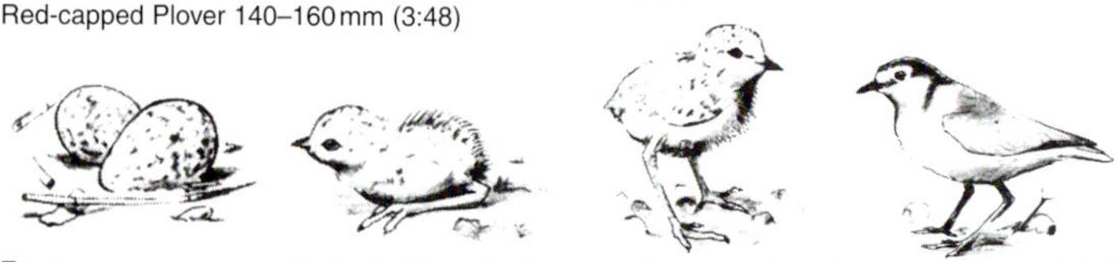

Eggs | Newly hatched chick | Ten-day old chick | Adult

52 BROAD-BILLED SANDPIPER *Limicola falcinellus* 160–180mm
Medium-small, short-necked, short-legged wader with long, straight, flattened bill. Active, continually probing into mud, crouching when disturbed. Buzzing trill call. Breeds in N Europe. Regular visitor in small numbers to specific localities in south.

53 TEREK SANDPIPER *Xenus cinereus* 220–240mm
Medium-sized, orange-legged wader with long up-curved bill. Strong flight, skimming low over water. Rising call 'twit-twit-twit-twit'. Active, chasing prey on water surface. Breeds in N Russia. Several records in SE, more common in north.

54 PECTORAL SANDPIPER *Calidris melanotos* 190–230mm
Similar to but larger than Sharp-tailed Sandpiper, yellow legs, longer neck and slightly decurved bill. Musical chirping call. Zig-zagging flight like snipe. Brown head and neck, clearly demarcated from white underparts. Breeds in N Russia and N America. Regular but rather rare visitor to SE.

55 ORIENTAL PRATINCOLE *Glareola maldivarum* 230–240mm
General: Olive-brown above, grey-buff to white below. Short black-forked white tail; legs dark grey; pale throat margined by thin black line. **Behaviour:** Plover-like running with head-bobbing, stopping to stand upright. Fly high, hawking for insects. 'Chik-chik', churring and soft 'tweet' calls. **Distribution:** Breed in S Asia, migrating to N Aust Nov–Feb. Nomadic, small flocks in dry country of SE Aust.

56 BUFF-BREASTED SANDPIPER *Tryngites subruficollis* 180–210mm
Medium-small, plover-like sandpiper with plump body and yellowish legs. Buff wash on breast with fine black spots. Usually feed alone in crouched position. Plover-like flight; soft growling call. Rare visitor to SE Aust, breeding in Alaska and N Russia.

57 WHITE-RUMPED SANDPIPER *Calidris fuscicollis* 150–170mm
Medium-small, long-winged wader keeping low horizontal profile at rest. In flight, a distinctive white band above tail. Call a mouse-like squeak. Often with other sandpipers. Breeds in N America. Very rare visitor to SE Aust.

ASSOCIATED WILDLIFE

 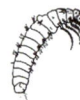  

Caddis Fly 25mm   Larva 20mm   Water Beetle 25mm   Larva 25mm

(58) COMMON SANDPIPER *Actitis hypoleucos* 190–220 mm
General: Medium-small sandpiper with long body and short yellow-green legs; brown, finely-barred upperparts with dark breast clearly demarcated from white abdomen. Plaintive 'twee-twee-tweee' call. Often solitary, perching on rocks and branches. Flies low to water. Breeds across Eurasia. **Distribution:** Scattered regular records around Aust coastal and inland waterways.

(59) BLACK–TAILED GODWIT *Limosa limosa* 360–430 mm
General: Medium-large slender wader with long legs and long straight pink bill, pale eyebrow. Prominent white wing-bar evident in flight. Single 'kek' call or 'weeta-weeta-weeta'. Breeds N Europe through to N China. **Distribution:** Very rare. Single scattered records through SE Aust.

(60) WOOD SANDPIPER *Tringa glareola* 200–230 mm
General: Medium-sized grey-brown wader with long straight bill, dark line through eye, white eyebrow and white abdomen; long yellow-green legs. Active in shallow freshwater, among dead timber. Breeds in N Eurasia. **Distribution:** Uncommon across S Aust.

(61) LITTLE CURLEW *Numenius minutus* 300–360 mm
General: Similar to Eastern Curlew (3:56) but much smaller and with shorter, slightly down-curved bill with pink base; lightly streaked underparts. Voice a rapid 'tit-tit-tit-tit' or 'tchew-tchew-tchew'. Breeds in Siberia. **Distribution:** Scattered records around SE coast; moderately common in north.

(62) WILSON'S PHALAROPE *Steganopus tricolor* 220–240 mm
General: Medium-sized grey and white wader with black needle-like bill, small head and yellowish legs. Sits high in water, spinning and dipping to stab at insects; lurches after food on land. Breeds in S Canada and W US. **Distribution:** Very rare, a few single records from Vic.

(63) ASIAN DOWITCHER *Limnodromus semipalmatus* 330–360 mm
General: Like small godwit with very long dark bill swollen at tip; shorter dark legs; rump and tail white, finely barred black. Yelping call. Swift, powerful flight. Breeds in central and E Siberia. **Distribution:** Very rare. Scattered records in NSW and Vic.

Other rare visitors to our region include the Short-billed Dowitcher and the Ringed Plover.

RARER LOCAL WADERS

64 PAINTED SNIPE *Rostratula benghalensis* 240–300 mm
General: Medium-sized, long decurved brown bill. Female head, neck, breast brown, tinged black. White eye-stripe; 'V' on back and head-stripe buff; wings olive brown barred black. Legs greenish, iris brown. Male paler. **Nest:** Grass-lined depression in ground, close to water, among rushes; 4 cream eggs, finely lined black. Female mates with several males. Aug–Dec in south; leaving male to incubate eggs and rear young. **Behaviour:** Nomadic, singly, family groups or larger post-breeding flocks probing for insects in mud on edge of swamps. Well camouflaged. Moves, stands with head tucked into chest. Male chirps, female hisses. Slow deliberate flight. **Distribution:** Rare. Critically endangered. Spasmodic appearances, responding to rainfall, some moving north in winter. Not recorded Tas.

65 HOODED PLOVER *Thinornis rubricollis* 190–230 mm
General: Shy, medium-small, buff-grey, white nape and underparts; distinctive black head, throat and side tail-feathers. Eye-ring red; bill orange, tipped black; legs pink; immature pale crown, white around face, brown line from beak to below eye. Head of female brown-black. **Nest:** Depression in sand among stones and shells. 2–3 stone-colored eggs heavily spotted purplish-black. Aug–Jan. **Behaviour:** Sedentary. Usually pairs or small groups on less frequented ocean beaches. Short, plaintive whistle, deep 'fow-fow'; barking, piping or 'querk-querk' calls. Walk slowly away from intruders. Swift flight. **Distribution:** Rare, open beaches of S Aust. Numbers decreasing.

66 BANDED LAPWING *Vanellus tricolor* 250–280 mm
General: Brown back and wings; underparts white, but black on cap extends down to prominent breast band. White mark through eye; small red wattle above yellow bill. White bar across wings obvious in flight. **Nest:** Grass-lined scrape; 3–4 olive-green eggs, spotted brown, mainly Jun–Oct. **Behaviour:** Clipped wing-beats; strident 'kew-kew-kew' or 'a-chee-chee-chee' calls. Small flocks on open ground like ploughed paddocks, eating seeds, invertebrates. **Distribution:** Widespread, uncommon across south, including Tas.

SIMILAR SPECIES	ASSOCIATED WILDLIFE

Bush Stone-curlew 550–590 mm (5:22)	Scarab Larva 35 mm

OCEAN AND BEACHES

67 STRIATED HERON *Butorides striatus* 430–510 mm
General: Stocky, black-capped, short neck; grey and rufous colour phases. Grey phase mostly seen Aust E coast, head and nape greenish-black, upperparts grey with green tinge; underparts brownish with white streaks under neck. **Voice:** Usually silent; utters loud squawk if disturbed. **Flight:** Slow, laborious, direct. **Food:** Marine life in mangroves. **Nest:** Frail platform of loose sticks in mangrove or nearby tree. 2–3 bluish-green eggs. Spring. **Behaviour:** Usually solitary; feeds on mudflats, mangrove swamps and along banks of coastal rivers. Occasionally dives into water from perch on tree. Head hunched over back, ready to dart out and catch prey; if approached stretches upright, with bittern-like camouflage. **Distribution:** Common along E coast.

68 EASTERN REEF EGRET *Egretta sacra* 600–700 mm
General: Large, white phase more frequently in north. Grey phase dark slaty-grey, white under neck. Skin around eye yellow; bill brownish, legs greenish. Nuptial plumes on neck during breeding. **Voice:** Harsh, loud croaking when disturbed. **Flight:** Heavy, direct with head tucked back over body. **Food:** Small marine animals: molluscs, crustacean, fish, etc. **Nest:** Stick platform on rock-ledge, small tree or shrub near ocean. 2–3 pale bluish eggs, warmer months in south. **Behaviour:** Singly or in pairs, along coasts, flying low over water, stalking prey in shallows and rock pools, or perching on rocks or trees near beach with head hunched. **Distribution:** Moderately common Aust coastline, absent from Vic, contracting along SA coast. **Similar species:** White-faced Heron 660–700 mm (4:48).

69 INTERMEDIATE EGRET *Ardea intermedia* 560–700 mm
General: Slender, white, long neck and dark legs. Plumes on back. Upper legs and yellow bill turn red when breeding. **Behaviour:** Often form large flocks. Hunt by standing and waiting, gleaning or foot-stirring with neck extended, looking for fish and frogs. Usually silent, croaking calls at colonial nesting sites in coastal or inland swamps. Stick platform nest in mangroves, casuarinas, melaleucas, etc; 3–4 pale green eggs. Nov–Apr. **Distribution:** Widespread, rarer in south; critically endangered in Vic.

white phase

70 OSPREY *Pandion haliaetus* 500–650mm
General: Large brown and white crested hawk with long, feathered legs and large claws. Upperparts mottled sooty-brown; head and neck white with brown streaks; brown stripe through eye; underparts mottled brown and white. Male smaller. **Voice:** Sad, drawn-out 'pee-ee, pee-ee'. **Flight:** Slow, deliberate, with bowed wings. Plunges from height to catch prey, sometimes going underwater. **Food:** Live fish or carrion, picked up with claws. **Nest:** Large stick platform lined with seaweed; on cliffs, lighthouses, mangroves and larger trees. Nest often added to over years until quite tall. 2–3 dull white eggs blotched reddish-purple. May–Sept. **Behaviour:** Singly or in pairs, usually along coastlines, estuaries, occasionally inland rivers; perched in trees, on rocks or hunting high above water. **Distribution:** Occurs almost worldwide. Moderately common along Aust coastline; but rare along Vic and S NSW coasts; absent from Tas.

71 GREY GOSHAWK *Accipiter novaehollandiae* 400–540mm
General: Medium-large, greyish, underparts white, finely barred breast. Female (average 680g) larger than male (average 350g). Rarer white phase in Tas, Otway Ranges in Vic and NW Aust. **Voice:** Clear, pleasant call with upward note at end, repeated several times. **Flight:** Swift, direct when chasing prey; slower when seeking food. Often seen soaring across valleys. **Food:** Large insects (grasshoppers, cicadas, beetles), small birds, reptiles and mammals, either caught on ground or in flight. **Nest:** Large stick platform; lined with green leaves, usually high in eucalypt. Occasionally uses old raven's nest. 2, rarely 3, pale bluish-white eggs. Aug–Dec. White and grey phases interbreed, phase of bird discernible on hatching. **Behaviour:** Singly or in pairs. Nomadic. Extremely wary of humans. Shakes tail sideways when alighting. Prey secured with rapid dive. **Distribution:** Moderately common in coastal forest.

SIMILAR SPECIES	ASSOCIATED WILDLIFE	

Brown Goshawk 400–500mm (2:46)	Antechinus 140mm	Mullet 760mm

OCEAN AND BEACHES

white phase

⑦⓪

⑦①

43

Birds of the southern plains and heaths

72 GROUND PARROT *Pezoporus wallicus* 280–330 mm
General: Medium-sized, greenish, long-tailed, terrestrial bird blotched yellow and black; red spot on forehead. Immature birds lack head spot. **Voice:** Soft, musical 'tigit-tigit'. **Flight:** Swift, erratic, low and usually short; yellow wing-stripe prominent. **Food:** Seeds of herbaceous plants, grasses, etc. **Nest:** Depression under tussock or shrub, lined with grasses. 2–3 rounded white eggs. Sept–Nov. Newly hatched chicks covered in black down. **Behaviour:** Usually singly or in pairs. Very shy and secretive; if flushed bursts from heath, usually landing nearby, but difficult to flush again. Numbers appear to peak 3–4 years after a fire, if burning not too frequent. **Distribution:** Very rare, threatened by habitat destruction and predation. In isolated pockets from Otway Ranges to Brisbane on coastal and nearby tableland heaths; moderately common W Tas. Probably extinct in SA and re-discovered in WA in 1993.

73 ROCK PARROT *Neophema petrophila* 210–230 mm
Dull green grass-parrot with blue facial mask and blue-edged wing. Stands upright, ascends rapidly when flushed. Feeds among rocks and samphire flats. Nests among rocks; 4–5 glossy rounded white eggs. Sept–Dec. Rare. Sedentary. Confined to WA and SA where they breed mostly on off-shore islands. Visits nearby coasts in autumn.

74 MULGA PARROT *Psephotus varius* 250–310 mm
Medium-sized green and blue parrot with yellow forehead and shoulder, red nape and belly-patch. Female duller. In flight female and immature show pale wing-bars. Distinctive 'wit-wit' flight call. Nests in hole in tree, 4–6 white eggs. Aug–Jan. In pairs or family flocks. Rather rare, inland scrubs and along watercourses.

75. ELEGANT PARROT *Neophema elegans* 220–240mm

General: Medium-sized, long-tailed green and yellow parrot with bluish shoulders. Upperparts olive-green, forehead and upper tail blue; face, throat and underparts yellow with greenish tinge on breast. Eye dark brown, legs grey and beak grey-brown. Sexes similar but female is duller. Immature lack blue forehead. **Voice:** Rather musical 'tsit', usually uttered in flight; soft twitter while feeding. **Flight:** Typical 'blue-winged parrot' flight; short, fluttering and erratic, flies to nearby tree if disturbed feeding. Rapid and direct over longer distances. **Food:** Seeds and other plant material collected on the ground. **Nest:** Hole in tree at varying heights above ground. 4–5 round white eggs. Aug–Nov. **Behaviour:** Usually in small flocks, feeding on ground in open savanna or coastal scrub in more arid parts of Aust. Often seen running rapidly from one grass clump to another. Species is possibly nomadic, at least on edges of its range. **Distribution:** Moderately common to common in SA. Rare in W Vic and SW NSW. Numbers fluctuate with season and food availability.

76. ORANGE-BELLIED PARROT *Neophema chrysogaster* 200–220mm

General: Medium-sized parrot with blue shoulders and long blue tail. Upperparts bright grass green with blue forehead band; yellow face, abdomen and under tail. Orange patch on abdomen. Sexes similar, immatures duller with smaller abdominal patch. **Voice:** Soft twitter uttered in flight: if disturbed a distinctive 'buzzing' is heard. **Flight:** Typical 'Blue-winged Parrot' flight, rapid and direct with short glide at end. **Food:** Seeds and other plant material, grasses and coastal scrub vegetation. **Nest:** Hole in old eucalypt; 3–6 white eggs on rotting wood. Nov–Feb. **Behaviour:** Usually singly or in pairs on coastal grasslands, scrub or tidal flats, quietly feeding on ground, mainly in salt marsh. Has been observed in flocks of Blue-winged Parrots. Very closely related to Elegant Parrot. **Distribution:** Migratory across Bass Strait, recorded from coastal W Vic, Bass Strait Islands and Tas. Very rare; endangered. Recent studies suggest population less than 200 birds.

SIMILAR SPECIES	ASSOCIATED WILDLIFE
Blue-winged Parrot 200–230mm (2:40)	Glasswort

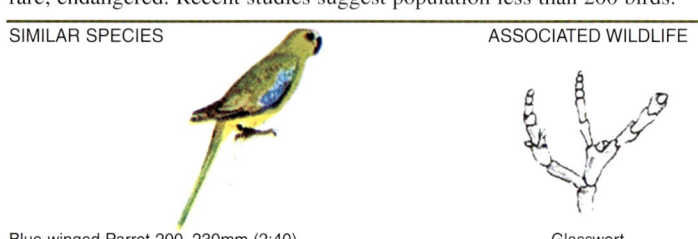

SOUTHERN PLAINS AND HEATHS

(77) **AUSTRALIAN BUSTARD** *Ardeotis australis* 760–1500 mm

General: Very large ground-dweller. Upper body mottled brown with black wing-stripe; head, neck and underparts whitish, black crown and chest-band. Male larger, darker wing than female. **Voice:** Usually silent; during breeding display male utters deep booming 'hoo'. **Flight:** Strong, slow; low over plain. Reluctant to fly, runs from danger. Flight preceded by long take-off run. **Food:** Omnivorous; mainly seeds and fruits, also insects, small reptiles and mammals. **Nest:** Hollow in ground, sometimes under bush; occasionally lined with sticks. Usually 1, sometimes 2 greenish eggs, marked with brown spots and blotches. Jun–Nov; determined by local rainfall. Chick independent shortly after hatching. **Behaviour:** Singly or in small flocks, feeding on grassland or open forest and scrub. Very confiding, inquisitive, often relying on camouflage to escape detection. Wary of humans but ignores cars. Male exhibits spectacular pre-breeding display; expanding neck and neck feathers, dropping wings and elevating tail as he struts around or stands still, booming. Nomadic, responding to rainfall variations. **Distribution:** Very rare in SE Aust; considered endangered, but still moderately common in northern and inland Aust. Species has suffered from habitat destruction, introduced predators and shooting. Protected in all states.

(78) **GRASS OWL** *Tyto capensis* 330–380 mm

General: Medium-large brownish terrestrial owl; similar to but darker than Barn Owl, longer legs. Upperparts dusky brown with lighter flecks, underparts buff with darker spots; long legs have no feathers. Large white facial disc edged with brown, brown patch in front of eye. Iris brown, legs and beak yellowish white. Female larger. **Voice:** Harsh rasping screeches, hissing scream, high-pitched cricket like contact call. **Flight:** Silent and slow. **Food:** Larger insects, smaller reptiles, rodents and marsupials. **Nest:** Under or in grass tussock, lined with grass. 4 oval white eggs, breeding depending on season. **Behaviour:** Usually singly. Nocturnal hunter, roosting on ground in grass clump, etc, during the day when it is difficult to flush. If flushed flies some distance, legs trailing behind, and plummets into tussocks again. **Distribution:** Rare. Coastal and near coastal heaths, swamps and inland grasslands; mainly coastal regions of NSW. Few records Vic and SA following mouse plagues; not in Tas.

SIMILAR SPECIES

Barn Owl 300–400 mm (7:60)

ASSOCIATED WILDLIFE

Fringe-myrtle

Grasshopper 45 mm

SOUTHERN PLAINS AND HEATHS

QUAIL CHARACTERISTICS

Quail-like birds belong to three distinct families that have separately evolved. Stubble, Brown and King Quails are related to the pheasants, domestic fowls and turkeys and have four toes. Button-quails, which have only three toes, include the Painted, Little and Red-chested Button-quails, and are related to the cranes, rails and bustards. The Plains-wanderer, which resembles the bustard-quails but has a fourth (hind) toe, is related to the waders. Most quails nomadic, and numbers fluctuate depending on the season. Several species rarely seen, due either to shyness or depletion of numbers through habitat destruction, depredation by introduced predators (especially cats, foxes and dogs) and shooting.

(79) **KING QUAIL** *Coturnix chinensis* 120–150 mm
General: Small, brownish, ground-frequenting, short tail. Male upperparts blackish brown streaked black and white; black throat with prominent white cheeks and crescent-shaped band. Underparts slate-grey with chestnut abdomen. Iris red, beak black, legs yellow. Female upperparts dark brown streaked white; underparts lighter with black barring. Eye-stripe buff; throat white. Iris brown. **Voice:** Mournful high pitched 3-note whistle 'whit-too-whit', at night or early morning. **Flight:** Reluctant, weak, direct; flies with 'tail-heavy' appearance. Usually flushes close to intruder, bursting from cover. **Food:** Seeds of grasses and other plants, insects. **Nest:** Depression in ground, lined with grass; usually in shelter of shrubs or dense tussocks. 4–5 pale brown eggs well covered with fine blackish spots. Mainly summer. **Behaviour:** Usually in family parties or small flocks in dense cover around swamps, coastal scrub and neglected paddocks, rarely seen, shy, secretive, difficult to flush. Probably sedentary in most areas of range but nomadic when season unfavourable. **Distribution:** Endangered. Very rare scattered populations in Vic, NSW, Qld, mainly coastal and near-coastal heaths and swamplands. No recent records for SA.

(80) **RED-BACKED BUTTON-QUAIL**
Turnix maculosa 120–150 mm
Small. Yellowish bill, white eye; rusty-red collar; black spots on buff flanks. Mid to N coast of NSW, widespread in Top End. Nest hollow under tussock. 2–4 glossy pale grey eggs. Oct–Feb. Very rare.

81) RED-CHESTED BUTTON-QUAIL *Turnix pyrrhothorax* 120–160mm

General: Small, greyish brown, pale reddish-brown underparts. Female upperparts generally dark brownish, back flecked with black and buff, lighter tones on wings. Underparts distinctly lighter (giving bird 2-tone appearance), reddish breast. Male lighter in colouring and smaller. **Voice:** Quick rattling chatter as well as soft 'oom'. **Flight:** Reluctant flyer. Rapid, direct, keeping close to ground for short distance. **Food:** Mainly seeds, occasionally insects. **Nest:** Depression in ground, scantily lined with grasses under tussock or low shrub. 4 buffish-white eggs heavily marked with grey, red and brown spots and blotches. Oct–Mar, probably determined by rainfall. **Behaviour:** Usually in pairs or family groups (coveys) in dense grasslands and paddocks. Very rarely sighted. Reluctant to fly, often allowing themselves to be picked up when discovered. **Distribution:** Very rare throughout E Aust; apparently nomadic throughout range, especially in S areas. W slopes of Great Divide in NSW, Murray-Darling Basin. Few records Vic; occasional sightings SA.

82) PLAINS-WANDERER *Pedionomus torquatus* 150–190mm

General: Medium-small, spotted, resembling Button-quails but with small hind toe. Body mainly dark brown, barred black; underparts paler, black and white collar, chestnut breast. Female larger, brighter in colouring than male. **Voice:** Low pitched, penetrating 'oom'. Heard both day and night. **Flight:** Reluctant; preferring to run rather than fly. If flushed rises from ground, dips then flutters like young bird. **Food:** Seeds and insects, collected from ground. **Nest:** Depression in ground, lined with grass; usually in shelter of grass tussock or low shrub. 4 light stone-coloured eggs marked with darker tones of brown or grey. Sept–Feb depending on season. **Behaviour:** Usually singly or in pairs on open, dry savanna; on ground, low twig or bush. Often stands and runs with head outstretched and on tiptoe. Freezes if disturbed. **Distribution:** Sedentary, or nomadic, depending on food supply. Rare, critically diminishing in numbers as native habitat is reduced and feral cats, foxes, etc, increase. N and W Vic; inland NSW and E SA.

SIMILAR SPECIES	ASSOCIATED WILDLIFE

Little Button-quail 120–140mm (7:36)	New Holland Daisy

83 EASTERN BRISTLEBIRD *Dasyornis brachypterus* 200–220 mm
General: Medium-sized, long-tailed shy bird with glossy brown plumage. Upperparts reddish-brown, throat pale grey; rest of underparts greyish-brown with grey spots on breast. Prominent bristles around gape. **Voice:** Loud, melodious and often sustained. Varied series of repeated whistles, often ventriloquial. Also mimics other species. **Flight:** Reluctant, weak and short, usually direct, from one clump of scrub to another. **Food:** Mainly insects and a few seeds, collected from ground litter. **Nest:** Dome shaped with side entrance; of dry leaves and coarse grasses lined with finer materials, built close to ground in tussock, sword-grass or shrub. 2 very pale brown eggs dotted with darker tones. Aug–Dec. **Behaviour:** Usually in pairs, in dense heathland vegetation. Very shy, more often heard than seen. Its short wings and preference for running rather than flying gives it a mouse-like appearance as it moves across ground. When feeding tail is often erect and fanned. **Distribution:** Sedentary. Rare in isolated and discontinuous areas along eastern coast and coastal ranges of Aust, from Brisbane to far E Gippsland.

84 RUFOUS BRISTLEBIRD *Dasyornis broadbenti* 240–270 mm
General: Shy, medium-sized brownish bird with longish tail. Head rich rufous with pale face patch. Throat and breast pale grey with darker scalloping. Upperparts olive-grey, tail brownish. Sexes similar. **Voice:** Clear, penetrating succession of 3 or 4 notes, often ending in whip-like crack. Call frequently answered by male. Also series of clicks and squeaks. Often only indication of birds presence. **Flight:** Reluctant, weak and short. Prefers to run through dense undergrowth. **Food:** Terrestrial invertebrates, seeds and berries in litter and fallen trees. **Nest:** Large, domed; with conspicuous side tunnel leading from broad platform of rushes and fine grasses and rootlets. Built near ground in dense vegetation. 2 pale pink eggs marked purplish-grey on larger end, spotted all over with darker tones. Sept–Dec. **Behaviour:** Usually in pairs in dense coastal heaths and gullies. Very shy. Long tail is often raised and fanned. If briefly glimpsed running through undergrowth could be easily mistaken for small animal or female Blackbird. **Distribution:** Sedentary. Very rare in suitable habitats from Cape Otway, Vic to Murray R mouth, SA. Species threatened by fire and habitat destruction.

ASSOCIATED WILDLIFE

Swamp Paperbark

Clematis

Native Raspberry

SOUTHERN PLAINS AND HEATHS

85 BEAUTIFUL FIRETAIL *Stagonopleura bella* 115–130mm
General: Shy, inconspicuous; dark olive-brown above, grey underparts, both completely covered with fine, black barring. Bill and rump red, black around eye. **Voice:** Low plaintive whistle. **Flight:** Undulating, low, short. **Food:** Seeds, berries and insects. **Nest:** Neat bottle-shaped with opening at side; of grasses and few leaves; in dense-foliaged bush or low tree. 5–8 white eggs, Sept–Jan. **Behaviour:** Pairs or small parties in thick scrub and rushes near water, feeds on ground or perches on fences or bushes. If surprised runs 'mouse-like' through tussocks, or takes off with whirr of wings. **Distribution:** Coastal and range areas of SE Aust from S Qld to Eyre Peninsula in SA. Rare in Vic. Locally common in Tas.

86 PLUM-HEADED FINCH *Neochmia modesta* 105–115mm
General: Very small, brown, purple-plum forehead, pale cheeks. Underparts white with strong brown barring; back and white-spotted wings brown; black tail tipped white. Male dark plum-coloured chin; female white eyebrow. **Behaviour:** Ground-forager, seed-eater, small noisy flocks, climbing grass stems; strong undulating flight. Small rounded grass nest with side entrance in tall grass or low shrub; 4–7 white eggs; Sept–Jan. 'Tleep' call. **Distribution:** E Aust in from coast from Rockhampton to ACT. Migrates north in winter. Locally common. Rare in SE Aust.

87 NUTMEG MANNIKIN *Lonchura punctulata* 105–115mm INTRODUCED
General: Very small, brown, darker brown face, pale cinnamon-brown scaly underparts. **Behaviour:** Forages in grasses, climbing stems of wiry herbs, forbs and cereal grasses. Favours wastelands, lantana thickets. Perches on fence wires, flicking wings, swinging tail. Bottle-shaped nest of grass, leaves and bark in shrub or small tree. 4–5 white eggs. Sept–Dec. **Distribution:** Native of SE Asia. Aviary escapee. Moderately common and widespread along E coast from Townsville to Bega. Occasionally Canberra, Adelaide and Melbourne.

88 DOUBLE-BARRED FINCH *Taeniopygia bichenovii* 100–110mm
General: Very small, brown-backed, white face, black tail; strikingly marked with thin black bars under throat and across white breast. Eastern race white rump; northern black. **Behaviour:** Small flocks, foraging among seeding grasses; short undulating flight to cover. Bottle-shaped grass nest in grass, shrub, fenceposts, old nests of other birds. 4 or 5 white eggs. Jul–Dec. 'Tyaart-tyaart' call. **Distribution:** Moderately common, nomadic. N and E Aust to as far south as NE Vic.

SOUTHERN PLAINS AND HEATHS

Birds of the wetlands

89) MAGPIE GOOSE *Anseranas semipalmata* 750–900mm
General: Large, black and white. Beak reddish, legs yellow with toes only partially webbed. Immature white diffused with grey and brown. **Voice:** Loud, resonant honk; repeated several times. **Flight:** Strong, slow, deliberate. **Food:** Mainly foliage, seeds, bulbs of aquatic and terrestrial plants. **Nest:** Large floating mound of vegetation usually near centre of swamp. 4–14 creamy-white eggs; breeding determined by rainfall. **Behaviour:** Nomadic, in various sized, noisy flocks (groups of 5,000 are common in N Aust, dispersing into feeding groups of 200–300 birds). Small vagrant non-breeding flocks occur in south. When feeding, birds confiding, easily approached. **Distribution:** Common tropical Aust on coastal floodplains. Rare in south. Small numbers re-introduced into Vic.

90) CAPE BARREN GOOSE *Cereopsis novaehollandiae* 750–900mm
General: Large, grey, lighter grey on head, dark spots on wings; edges of wings and tail black. **Voice:** Quiet on ground, in flight utters series of grunts and honks. **Flight:** Slow, strong, direct. **Food:** Leaves, seeds of grasses, sedges and other plants. **Nest:** Grass mat, lined with down, either in depression among grass or on dense shrub up to 4m above ground. 4–6 white eggs May–Dec. **Behaviour:** Nomadic; wary, in small flocks, usually seen in summer grazing in paddocks, swamp edges and coastal grasslands. Very pugnacious in defence of nest and young. **Distribution:** Rare through coastal S Aust. Most breed on 6 island groups in Bass Strait.

91) BLACK-NECKED STORK *Ephippiorhynchus asiaticus* 1400–2000mm
General: Tall, black and white, massive, slightly-upturned bill, long red legs. **Behaviour:** Strides through shallows, running after fish with wings raised. **Flight:** Strong flight with slow wingbeats. **Nest:** Stick and grass platform in dead tree. 2–4 white eggs. Oct–Mar. **Distribution:** Occasionally sighted along E coast and N NSW.

WETLANDS

(92) FRECKLED DUCK *Stictonetta naevosa* 480–580mm
General: Large, freckled brown and white. Greenish-black upturned bill, base of male bill turns red in breeding season. **Voice:** Generally quiet; occasionally series of grunts, whistles and resonating roars. **Flight:** Fast distinctive wing-beat with head down, keeping low, circling before landing. **Food:** Filter feeder of aquatic vegetation; seeds of waterplants, algae on logs. **Nest:** Old coot nest or bowl-shaped platform of reeds, piled with downy feathers. Sometimes in tree over water or on flood debris. 5–7 greenish-white eggs. Sept–Dec. **Behaviour:** Nomadic. Usually a few in flocks of other ducks; occasional large flocks. Rarely seen flying, resting during day in reedbeds or perching on posts or stumps projecting from water. **Distribution:** Rather rare S Aust.

(93) PLUMED WHISTLING-DUCK *Dendrocygna eytoni* 400–620mm
General: Large. Long plumes on flanks. Pink legs, patchy pink bill. **Voice:** Shrill musical twitter. High-pitched whistling heard continuously in flight. **Flight:** Slow dangling legs with head held low; wings or plumes make whistling noise. **Food:** Herbivorous: grazing or dabbling. **Nest:** Hollow in ground, lined with dried grasses; often far from water. 8–12 glossy creamy-white eggs. Sept–Dec. **Behaviour:** Small flocks or pairs, often perching in rows on tree limbs or along water's edge. Plumes give bird military appearance. Grazing on pasture and native rushes, often far from camp and sometimes with wandering whistling-ducks. **Distribution:** Migratory. Moderately common in northern wetland and grasslands; rare in SE wetlands; usually only in wetter years.

(94) WANDERING WHISTLING-DUCK *Dendrocygna arcuata* 550–610mm
General: Lower profile in water than Plumed Whistling-Duck and with shorter flank plumes and darker crown, nape and back. Lacks fine breast barring. Dark legs and bill. **Voice:** Shrill descending whistle; twittering. In flight, whirring whistle of wings. **Flight:** Slow beat on rounded wings. **Food:** Flowers and seeds of aquatic plants. **Nest:** Scrape in ground; lined with grass. 6–8 cream eggs; Jan–May. **Behaviour:** Flocks feed in unison, dabbling and diving; in flight trailing birds move to head of flock. **Distribution:** N Aust and along E coast to as far south as Newcastle where only occasionally sighted.

ASSOCIATED WILDLIFE

Nardoo

Swamp Lily

Red Water-milfoil

95. LITTLE BITTERN *Ixobrychus minutus* 250–360mm
General: Medium-sized, secretive. Female duller. **Voice:** Low, soft booming, croaking call. **Flight:** Slow, deliberate, usually at night. Buff wing patches prominent. **Food:** Mainly nocturnal feeder on aquatic animals, eggs and chicks. **Nest:** Platform of reeds, slung over water or on low trees in dense reed-beds. 4 white eggs. Spring. **Behaviour:** Nomadic. Very shy, skulking in freshwater reed-beds, either singly or in pairs. If disturbed birds often stand with necks stretched up. **Distribution:** Uncommon in SE Aust.

96. RUFF (♂) and REEVE (♀) *Philomachus pugnax* 200–320mm
General: Medium-sized, upright. Breeding plumage, rarely seen in Aust, sexes differ so much, were once considered to be different species. Male much larger. Eclipse plumage resembles that of Sharp-tailed Sandpiper (1:16). **Voice:** Silent when away from breeding areas. **Flight:** Fast, erratic. **Food:** Mainly aquatic animal life from swamp and lake margins; some seeds. **Behaviour:** Usually in mixed flocks with other waders. Breeding males develop elaborate neck frills. During non-breeding dispersal, when in Aust, sexes similar in appearance. **Distribution:** Very rare vagrant in Aust during southern summer. In SE Aust occasionally seen on coastal and inland marshes. Nests in N Eurasia, tended by male.

97. SPOTLESS CRAKE *Porzana tabuensis* 170–210mm
General: Medium-small, dark, with red legs. **Voice:** Sharp 'crik-crik', short grunting call. **Flight:** Reluctant; short, weak and fluttering with legs trailing. **Food:** Plants and insects, mainly aquatic. **Nest:** Loosely woven cup of grass; on small platform on ground or on tussock; close to, or above, water. 4–7 pale greenish-grey eggs marked brown. Oct–Jan. **Behaviour:** Usually singly, very shy and retiring; in dense grass, etc around fresh and saline swamps, mangroves and saltbush areas. When alarmed flicks tail rapidly. **Distribution:** Considered rare throughout Aust, NZ and nearby islands but may be more common. Not often sighted because of secretive habits.

---

96 SIMILAR SPECIES

Ruff 200–320mm (4:62) | Nankeen Night Heron 560–640mm (4:56) | Australian Spotted Crake 190–230mm (4:60) | Baillon's Crake 150–180mm (4:60)

Birds of the rainforests

98 BLACK-FACED MONARCH *Monarcha melanopsis* 160–190mm
General: Medium-small, active, migratory grey bird with black face and chin; brown tinge on wings and tail; rufous abdomen. Immature birds lack black face. **Voice:** Loud whistle-like 'why-yew, which-yew', also chattering 'fly-catcher' calls. **Food:** Insects and their larvae, mainly collected from leaves and branches; sometimes on wing. **Nest:** Deep, cup-shaped, camouflaged with, moss and lined with rootlets in fork of leafy tree up to 10m from ground. 2–3 white eggs, spotted red and purple. Summer. **Behaviour:** Singly or in pairs, mainly in densely timbered coastal rainforests and gullies. Noisily moving through foliage in search of food. **Distribution:** Rare throughout coastal E Aust. Summer migrant in south, permanent resident in north. Recorded as far west as Dandenong Ranges in Vic.

OTHER RARE FLYCATCHERS

Satin Flycatcher 150–170mm (2:74)   Leaden Flycatcher 140–160mm (2:74)

99 RED-TAILED BLACK-COCKATOO *Calyptorhynchus banksii* 500–640mm
General: Large, glossy black, prominent crest, broad sub-terminal tail-band. Female brownish black, yellow spots on head and wings. Yellow barring on breast, black bars on red tail-band. **Voice:** Loud, harsh 'kree-' or 'krurr-'. **Flight:** Heavy, slow, direct; from one tree clump to next, calling. Longer flights made at considerable height. **Food:** Seeds of banksias, casuarinas and eucalypts; nectar, insects and larvae (particularly wood-boring grubs). **Nest:** Hole in tree, usually high. 1–2 pure white eggs. **Behaviour:** Nomadic. Usually in noisy pairs or small parties in dense forests, open woodland or savanna areas. Often feed on ground. Shy, react noisily to any disturbance day or night with loud screeching. Large eucalypts along watercourse preferred as roosting sites. **Distribution:** Rather rare to rare in SA and W Vic. Decreasing in numbers.

100 GLOSSY BLACK-COCKATOO *Calyptorhynchus lathami* 460–510mm
General: Medium-large, smoky brown, long-tailed, black wings and back. No distinct crest. Male broad red tail-band, female yellow patches on head, fine black barring on red tail-band. Immature like female, but occasionally yellow wing-patches. Young males may have unbarred red tail-band. **Voice:** Soft double-call 'tarred, tarr-ed'. **Flight:** Heavy, slow, deliberate and direct, either through canopy or above it. Glides with down-curved wings. **Food:** Mainly seeds, especially Banksia and *Casuarina littoralis*. **Nest:** Hollow limb or hole in trunk; lined with fine wood chips; usually quite high above ground, in dead tree. 1 dull white egg. Spring. **Behaviour:** Almost completely arboreal. Nomadic pairs or family groups, sometimes flocks. Noisy clicking as layers peeled off casuarina cones to obtain seeds. Flocks often travel considerable distances between feeding localities. **Distribution:** Rare, apparently decreasing. Mountain, floodplain and coastal forests of E Aust from central Qld to Mitchell River, E Vic. Also on Kangaroo Island, SA.

SIMILAR SPECIES	ASSOCIATED WILDLIFE

Yellow-tailed Black-Cockatoo 550–650mm (2:42)   Black She-oak   White Stringybark

101 GREEN CATBIRD *Ailuroedus crassirostris* 240–320 mm
General: Stocky, bright green, powerful white bill, brown head, red eye, white eye-ring. Olive underparts, white spots on tips of wing-feathers. **Behaviour:** Small flocks in autumn, feeding on rainforest and orchard fruit. Cat-like calls or sharp 'tik'. Well camouflaged in canopy. Large open cup nest of vines, twigs, leaves and moss lined with bark. 2 white eggs. Sept–Feb. **Distribution:** E coastal forests from Gladstone, Qld to Royal National Park, NSW.

102 AUSTRALASIAN FIGBIRD *Sphecotheres viridis* 270–300 mm
General: Green race (coastal E Aust) Male grey-green throat and breast, white abdomen, dark head, red skin around eye, black-lined wings, black tail with white edges. Female dull olive-brown, pale underparts, heavily streaked brown, especially under throat. **Behaviour:** Small flocks; foraging in foliage of fruiting trees. Acrobatic, fluttering, hanging upsidedown, perching on overhead wires. Undulating flight; squeaky 'see-chew' or 'chock-yer' call. Hammock nest of vines and twigs in horizontal fork; 2–3 green eggs, spotted brown. Oct–Feb. **Distribution:** E coastal forests from Cape York to Nowra in NSW. Vagrant Vic.

103 COMMON KOEL *Eudynamys scolopacea* 400–460 mm
General: Medium-large cuckoo. Distinctive 'koo-ell', rising 'quoy-quoy-quoy-quoy' calls. Male glossy blue-black with red eye and white bill; female brown above, many white spots, dark crown and face, pale barred underparts. **Behaviour:** Feeds on fruits in leafy trees, preferring figs and mistletoes. Vocal day and night, especially during breeding. Lays 1 salmon-pink egg with wavy purplish streaks in nest of hosts like Magpie-larks, larger honeyeaters and orioles. **Distribution:** Summer migrant from Indonesia, arriving in north during The Wet. Moderately common along E coast to Vic border, occasionally central Vic.

104 REGENT BOWERBIRD *Sericulus chrysocephalus* 250–300 mm
General: Glossy, black and gold, thrush-like, yellow eye and bill. Female brown, flecked white, longer tail, black bill, black patch on nape. Male acquires full plumage after 5 years. **Behaviour:** Chattering, wheezing, rattling calls, sometimes ventriloquial. Also mimics. Fast, low and direct flight. Small avenue-type bower with parallel walls, decorated with snail shells, berries, leaves and seeds. Saucer nest high in rainforest creepers; 2 pale brown eggs, lined purple; Oct–Jan. **Distribution:** E ranges south to Royal National Park, NSW.

RAINFORESTS

105 SCARLET HONEYEATER *Myzomela sanguinolenta* 100–110 mm
General: Very small, active, black down-curved bill. Male head, back and breast scarlet. Female plain brown, darker above. Immature similar. **Voice:** Incessant musical tinkling, especially during breeding. **Flight:** Fast, erratic. **Food:** Mainly nectar, occasionally insects, some taken on wing. **Nest:** Frail, cup-shaped, bark and cobwebs; suspended by rim in fork of outer foliage; often close to ground. 2–3 whitish eggs lightly spotted yellow, red or purple on larger end. Oct–Jan. **Behaviour:** In pairs or groups in outer foliage of coastal forests, usually near streams. Nomadic, migratory in southern areas. **Distribution:** Coastal and near-coastal areas from N Qld to East Gippsland.

106 BROWN GERYGONE *Gerygone mouki* 90–110 mm
General: Very small, active, brown, pale grey underparts, prominent white eye-stripe. Tail indistinct dark sub-terminal band, tipped white. **Voice:** Melodious weak 'which-is-it, which-is-it', continuous while feeding. **Flight:** Short, rapid; often hovers near foliage or trunk while feeding. **Food:** Insects and larvae. **Nest:** Dome-shaped with long tail-piece; fibres decorated with moss, etc, bound with web; suspended from thin branch. Entrance spout-like, built near top. 2–3 reddish-white eggs freckled brown at larger end. Sept–Feb. **Behaviour:** Usually pairs; sometimes small flocks in cooler months; noisily moving through canopy and outer branches or methodically feeding on mossy trunks and branches of rainforest areas in associated coastal forest waterways. **Distribution:** Common pockets of coastal Qld, NSW. Rare in Gippsland.

107 LEWIN'S HONEYEATER *Meliphaga lewinii* 190–215 mm
General: Medium-small, olive-green, darker above, paler below. Face and head dark with pale yellow ear-patch and gape. **Voice:** Distinctive succession of loud, ringing, single notes. **Flight:** Fast, erratic. **Food:** Insects, introduced and native fruits; also nectar. **Nest:** Cup-shaped; fibres, etc held together with spider web, lined with finer materials; suspended by rim in thick foliage up to 7 m high. 2–3 white eggs marked reddish brown or darker tones. Sept–Jan. **Behaviour:** Sedentary flocks, aggressive, inquisitive; often with other fruit eating birds in canopy of rainforest and adjoining coastal scrub. **Distribution:** Rather rare. Coastal E Aust from N Qld to near Melbourne.

SIMILAR SPECIES

Western Gerygone 100–110 mm (p 104)

Brown Thornbill 90–115 mm (1:60)

RAINFORESTS

108 RED-BROWED TREECREEPER *Climacteris erythrops* 135–160mm
General: Small, insectivorous, brownish upperparts, slightly darker head. Face has buff wash; prominent reddish eyebrow. Female more red on face. Immature lacks reddish eye-stripe. **Voice:** Soft rapid high-pitched chatter, on one note. **Flight:** Rapid, undulating, from canopy of one tree to base of another. **Food:** Insects and larvae in and under bark. **Nest:** Cup-shaped, bark, fur and plant down in hollow spout, often high in dead trees, 3 purplish-red eggs. Aug–Jan. **Behaviour:** Pairs or small flocks, moving through higher rainfall forests of coastal and range areas. Feeds mostly in tree canopies. **Distribution:** Rather rare throughout entire range, S Qld to central Vic.

109 LARGE-BILLED SCRUBWREN *Sericornis magnirostris* 115–130mm
General: Small, active, yellowish brown above with lighter underparts and throat. Tawny-olive on forehead, around eye and on ear coverts. Bill black. **Voice:** Series of soft churring and scolding calls. **Flight:** Short, rapid, direct; from tree to tree. **Food:** Insects and their larvae obtained in foliage and on branches. **Nest:** Oval, with slightly hooded side entrance; of rootlets, leaf skeletons, vines, etc, lined with feathers and other soft material; in dense vine or foliage (eg, tree-fern). Renovates, occupies old nests of Yellow-throated Scrub-Wren. 3 greyish eggs finely spotted brown. Aug–Jan. **Behaviour:** Usually pairs or family groups, silently but actively searching for food in lower levels of denser range and coastal woodland. Prefers to feed on trunks, foliage, fallen branches and vines. Easily approached while feeding. **Distribution:** Moderately common in rainforests and coastal scrubs from Cooktown to S NSW. Rather rare in SE Vic.

110 FORTY-SPOTTED PARDALOTE *Pardalotus quadragintus* 90–100mm
General: Tiny, plain, olive-green, paler below with yellowish face, white-spotted black wings and white-tipped black tail. **Behaviour:** Feeds high in canopy of White (Manna) Gums on lerps and manna exudates. Monotonous high piping double-note call. Tree hollow nest of bark strips, grass, fur and feathers. 4 round white eggs; Aug–Dec. **Distribution:** Very rare. Confined to coastal SE Tas and adjacent islands.

111 **SPANGLED DRONGO** *Dicrurus bracteatus* 290–320mm
General: Medium-sized, glossy black, metallic green sheen on wings. Head, neck and breast spotted, iridescent blue-green. Eye red; legs and beak black; faint white spots on underwing, tail long, forked. **Voice:** Noisy, peculiar chattering call. Occasionally mimics other birds. **Flight:** Direct, short rapid flights after food. **Food:** Insects, usually caught on wing, also eats nectar and buds; attacking other birds. **Nest:** Open, cup-shaped, of vines and tendrils in horizontal fork, often at considerable height. 3–5 eggs, pale warm greys spotted by reddish tones. Oct–Feb. **Behaviour:** Usually singly or in small flocks, perching on higher limbs of trees fringing clearings in rainforest or mangroves; flies out to catch food, then returns to perch. Often nests in vicinity of friarbirds. Chases cuckoo-shrikes, Magpie-larks and Willie Wagtails, forcing them to release food. **Distribution:** Common in coastal N and E Aust. A rare summer migrant in Vic rainforest areas, Oct–Mar. Accidental Tas.

112 **CICADABIRD** *Coracina tenuirostris* 240–260mm
General: Aggressive, medium-sized. Male dark leaden grey, slightly speckled black and brown. Black eye-stripe and white spot underwing. Female grey-brown above, buff edges to wing feathers; underparts lighter. **Voice:** Loud, chirring or buzzing. Very penetrating, carrying distances of up to 1km. Also sharp 'cheep' or 'chuck'. **Flight:** Rapid, direct. **Food:** Large insects, including cicadas; and their larvae. **Nest:** Relatively small, cup-shaped, of dried twigs, bark, lichen and moss bound with cobwebs and camouflaged with lichen, built in high fork in foliage; single greenish-grey egg marked brown and lavender. **Behaviour:** Singly or in small parties moving through canopy of mountain and coastal forests, along crests and ridges. Very aggressive, particularly during nesting, driving away other birds and defending nest vigorously against human intruders. Migratory, during warmer months, particularly in S Aust. **Distribution:** Rather rare in coastal N and E Aust. Rare in mountain ranges and coastal valleys in S NSW and E Vic.

SIMILAR SPECIES			ASSOCIATED WILDLIFE

Black-faced Cuckoo-shrike 300–360mm (2:16)	White-winged Triller 170–200mm (2:18)	Common Starling 210–220mm (1:26)	Lilly-pilly

Birds of the ranges

113 REGENT HONEYEATER *Xanthomyza phrygia* 200–230 mm
General: Medium-sized, black, prominent off-white scaly pattern on body, yellowish wing and tail-stripes. Pale pink warty skin around eye. Female smaller. Immature duller with creamy bill. **Voice:** Distinctive, penetrating bell-like bubbling, trilling, mewing, metallic 'clink, clink, clink'. **Flight:** Swift, looping between distant trees, flits between canopies. **Food:** Nectar from outer blossoms in canopy; gleans lerps, manna and honey-dew. Chases insects. **Nest:** Usually high in crowns of tall trees; open, cup-shaped; of bark, rootlets and grasses adorned with bark. 2–3 salmon-buff eggs with purple spots; May–Mar. **Behaviour:** Small highly nomadic flocks, often in mistletoe blossom, eucalypts, banksias or fruit trees, darting out to catch flying insects. Aggressive when feeding. **Distribution:** Rare; endangered, spasmodic irruptions along Great Divide in Vic and NSW, associated with ironbark forests. Largest colonies Chiltern, Vic; Blue Mountains and Capertee Valley, NSW. Before 1960, moderately common in E Melbourne suburbs.

114 HELMETED HONEYEATER *Lichenostomus melanops cassidix* 170–220 mm
General: Endangered race of Yellow-tufted Honeyeater (2:30). Medium-small crested greenish honeyeater with bright yellow crown. Outer tail-feathers tipped white. Female smaller, crest less distinct. **Voice:** Varied; high pitched 'twit-twit' and a scolding 'churr-churr' are main calls. **Flight:** Typical honeyeater; fast, short and erratic. **Food:** Nectar, berries and insects, including scale. **Nest:** Cup-shaped, of bark and twigs lined with grass and down; suspended in foliage from horizontal branch. 2 pale pink eggs finely marked with red. Jul–Dec. **Behaviour:** In pairs or small parties feeding in foliage of Manna Gums, etc, along foothill creeks. Species shows aggressive territorial attitude towards some other species but may not be competing successfully with Bell Miner. **Distribution:** Very rare; critically endangered. Entire world population is about 200 birds in Dandenong Ranges, Vic—most at Yellingbo. Captive breeding program conducted by Healesville Sanctuary.

RANGES

115 BRUSH CUCKOO *Cacomantis variolosus* 220–260 mm
General: Medium-sized, brownish cuckoo, olive tint on back, head, shoulders, underparts grey with rufous tinge on breast. Brown tail notched white on outer edges of feathers. Young heavily mottled brown. **Voice:** Slow deliberate descending whistle of 6 to 8 notes. Sometimes heard at night. **Flight:** Short, rapid except when migrating. **Food:** Large variety of insects and their larvae, sometimes collected on ground. **Nest:** Egg laid in nest of other birds. Whitish eggs marked with purple. Recorded from nests of a variety of birds that build open, bowl-shaped structures (woodswallows, fantails, flycatchers, etc) in most months of the year in N Aust and during Oct–Jan in south. At least 30 species recorded as hosts for this cuckoo. **Behaviour:** Usually solitary. Inconspicuous bird mainly seen sitting quietly on branch in undergrowth and regrowth areas of open woodland and rainforests. **Distribution:** Common, sedentary in coastal N Aust, rarer and nomadic in south. Recorded as far west as Dandenong Ranges in Vic. **Similar Species:** Fan-tailed Cuckoo 250–270 mm (2:16).

116 WHITE-THROATED NIGHTJAR *Eurostopodus mystacalis* 320–370 mm
General: Medium-large nocturnal bird; upperparts mottled black, rufous and grey; white patches on sides of throat. Underparts finely barred rufous and dark brown. **Voice:** Harsh, repeated cackle; notes ascending scale. **Flight:** Silent, rapid, acrobatic. **Food:** Larger insects, caught on wing at dusk or night. **Nest:** No nest made, egg laid on ground among litter. Single stone coloured egg blotched with darker tones. Oct–Jan. **Behaviour:** Singly or in pairs on drier ridges of coastal and highland forest areas. During day roost on ground; relying on camouflage to escape detection. Often seen hawking just above ground and through trees in evening; or catching insects attracted to lights. Migratory, leaving S areas Feb–Apr; returning NSW in Sept and Nov in Vic. **Distribution:** Rare coastal forests and nearby areas of Great Divide, from Cape York to central Vic, where it occurs as far west as Otway Ranges.

SIMILAR SPECIES	NIGHTJAR WINGS

Spotted Nightjar 290–330mm
(p111 and 5:62); ranges partly overlap.

White-throated   Spotted

117 CHANNEL-BILLED CUCKOO *Scythrops novaehollandiae* 580–660 mm
General: Large, pale grey, big curved grey to straw-coloured bill; long tail, long pointed wings, barred tail with darker terminal band and white tip. Red skin around eye. Immature browner with cream underparts. **Voice:** Loud, repeated rising 'awk-awk-awk-awk' call; sometimes at night. Screeching 'cree-cree-cree', raucous 'ca-ca-ca-ca-ca', 'ee-yawk-ee-yawk'. **Flight:** Strong, direct, rigid wing-beats. **Food:** Fruit, seeds of native trees, insects, eggs and nestlings of other birds. **Behaviour:** 1–4 buff-coloured eggs with chestnut blotches in nests of currawongs, ravens, crows, choughs and magpies. Often harassed by other birds. **Distribution:** Widespread N and E Aust, as far south as Bega in NSW. Some records for E Vic, Tas.

118 PHEASANT COUCAL *Centropus phasianinus* 500–700 mm
General: Large, long-tailed, pheasant-like, dark breeding plumage, chestnut-coloured back, brown wings, darker brown tail barred white; red eye. Non-breeding paler brown white streaked body. **Voice:** Scale call, a rich, hollow, repeated 'oop-oop-oop-oop-oop-oop-oop…', slowing and descending. Also scolding 'keow', 'chuff-chuff', soft hooting. **Flight:** Short, laboured dashes, flopping into cover. **Food:** Large insects, frogs, mice, eggs and young of other birds. **Behaviour:** Skulks through or around dense cover, perches in crowns of low shrubs, lower foliage or on fenceposts. Sunbathes with wings and tail outspread. **Distribution:** Widespread across north, far south as the Hunter River, east of the Great Divide. Sedentary.

119 ORIENTAL CUCKOO *Cuculus saturatus* 280–330 mm
Uncommon but widespread Asian cuckoo visiting N Aust, as far south as Barren Grounds in coastal NSW. Grey head and chest, whitish underparts, barred black, yellow eyes and legs. Rufous form female dark barring on head and neck. Rapid 'bu-bu-bu-bu…' call. Feeds on caterpillars. Nov–May.

120 FORK-TAILED SWIFT *Apus pacificus* 160–190 mm

Uncommon Asian visitor to SE Aust during summer, preceding storm fronts and humid weather, when flying ants and termites emerge. Far outnumbered by similar White-throated Needletail. Numbers reversed in N and W mainland. Breed in central Asia.

121 SOOTY OWL *Tyto tenebricosa* 380–500 mm

General: Medium-large, dark, lighter underparts; covered with small white spots. Prominent rounded grey-white facial disc edged with black. Beak and eyes brown, legs greyish. Female larger. **Voice:** Usually silent, occasionally varied whistling screech or territorial descending call. **Flight:** Typical owl flight, silent, slow and direct. Prefers to fly at night. **Food:** Insects, smaller marsupials, rodents, etc. **Nest:** Hollow or hole in spout; usually high in tree. 3 white eggs; all year. **Behaviour:** Usually singly or in pairs well up in canopy of forest. Nocturnal hunter, roosting in hollow tree or dense foliage of forests during day. Very secretive, unobtrusive except for very vocal territorial defence during breeding in Lilly-pilly gullies of E Aust. **Distribution:** Sedentary. Rare, coastal forests from central Qld to W Gippsland

122 MASKED OWL *Tyto novaehollandiae* 330–550 mm

General: Medium-large, dark, varying plumage. Upperparts grey or brown with darker blotches and fine white spots; underparts white with rufous speckling. Distinct facial disc varies from white to light grey-brown, edged with brown. Like Barn Owl but darker, more boldly patterned. **Voice:** Loud screech, heard infrequently. **Food:** Insects, small reptiles, birds, mammals. **Flight:** Silent, direct, fairly fast. **Nest:** Hollow in tree, usually on high ground, 2–3 dull white oval eggs. Winter. **Behaviour:** Usually singly, or in pairs during breeding season. Nocturnal, roosting in dense foliage, in caves, concealed crevices. **Distribution:** Rare in SE Aust, more common in Tas.

123 POWERFUL OWL *Ninox strenua* 600–660 mm

General: Large brown nocturnal hunters; upperparts barred white; underparts buff-white barred brown. Female duller. **Voice:** Mournful, deep, 'woo-hoo'. Young have trilling call. **Flight:** Rapid, direct. **Food:** Marsupials, rodents, birds. Clutch partly eaten prey all day while roosting. **Nest:** Cavity, lined with wood-pulp; high in large tree, usually on steep, heavily-wooded slope. 2 roundish white eggs. May–Sept. **Behaviour:** Shy. Usually in pairs. Often roost short distance apart during day, in thick foliaged trees like blackwood wattles and pines. **Distribution:** Rare. Sparsely distributed most of SE and E Aust ranges, from north of Brisbane to SA–Vic border. In Vic mainly recorded south of Great Divide.

SIMILAR SPECIES	ASSOCIATED WILDLIFE
 Barn Owl 300–400 mm (7:60)	 Bush Rat *Rattus fuscipes* 350 mm

124. AUSTRALIAN KING PARROT *Alisterus scapularis* 410–440 mm
General: Medium-large, mainly arboreal, long bluish-black tail. Male, head and underparts scarlet, back and wings dark green with pale green band, rump blue, horn-coloured upper mandible. Female, generally dark green with red abdomen, dark bill; no pale wing-band. Immature male like female but red blotches on face and throat, pale bill and indistinct wing-band. **Flight:** Heavy, laboured, direct. **Voice:** Shrill metallic 'crassak-crassak', loud shrieks when disturbed. **Food:** Mainly seeds, fruits (including cultivated species), berries and nectar. **Nest:** Hollow in eucalypt, preferably in tall tree. Some nests found in trees with entrance over 10 m above ground with nest down near ground level. 3–5 white rounded eggs. Oct–Jan. **Behaviour:** Pairs or small flocks, usually seen feeding in outer branches of rainforest areas. Drinks and sometimes feeds on ground. In autumn immature in flocks of up to 30 birds. Courtship displays end in courtship feeding by male. **Distribution:** Nomadic throughout wetter Great Divide areas of E Aust, from Cooktown to Macedon Ranges and Otway Ranges. Some altitudinal migration reported. Moderately common to rather rare throughout range.

125. WONGA PIGEON *Leucosarcia melanoleuca* 360–400 mm
General: Shy, medium-large, terrestrial. Upperparts, chest dark slaty grey, white forehead and 'necklace'. Underparts mottled white and black. Red skin around eye. **Voice:** Loud 'woop-woop-woop', heard for long periods in breeding season. **Flight:** Short, straight and fast, usually from tree to tree. Reluctant to fly, but when flushed rises with loud clap of wings. **Food:** Mainly seeds, berries and other fruits, young plants: occasionally insects. **Nest:** Rough, fragile open platform of twigs on horizontal bough, often well above ground. 2 white eggs; mostly Aug–Jan. Possibly breeds twice in year. **Behaviour:** Singly or in pairs; occasionally small (family) flocks in dense forests and gullies. Bobs head continuously when walking. **Distribution:** Sedentary in coastal areas and adjacent ranges from Rockhampton to central Gippsland. Moderately common in northern states, rarer in SE.

SIMILAR SPECIES

adult   immature

Crimson Rosella 320–370 mm (2:42)

126 EMERALD DOVE *Chalcophaps indica* 230–280mm
General: Medium-sized dark pink-brown pigeon; iridescent dark green across back and on upperwings with white shoulder patch; black tail; bill and legs orange to purple. **Voice:** Low, single, penetrating 'ooo' note, repeated many times. **Flight:** Low, short swift and silent, weaving through trees; regular wing-beats with head raised. **Food:** Seeds, fallen fruits and some small invertebrates. **Nest:** Frail twig platform, 2–6m up in dense forest habitats; 2 cream-coloured eggs. Mostly Jun–Aug. **Behaviour:** Ground-feeder, usually in pairs. When flushed, fly rapidly along forest edge or track then dive in for safety. **Distribution:** Common along E coastal ranges to as far south as Shoalhaven River with some records in E Vic.

127 TOPKNOT PIGEON *Lopholaimus antarcticus* 400–450mm
General: Medium-large pale-grey pigeon with curious 'topknot' in front of ginger-coloured crown; dark-grey above with pale grey neck and underparts faintly streaked; dark grey tail with prominent white sub-terminal band; bill and feet deep pink. **Voice:** Low squeak and high-pitched 'cooo-oo, ooo'. **Flight:** Strong with glides, circling above rainforests. **Food:** Fruits of native rainforest trees and introduced Camphor Laurel. **Nest:** Stick platform on horizontal fork in canopy; 1 white egg, Oct–Dec. **Behaviour:** Usually in pairs or flocks (sometimes hundreds). Very acrobatic, hanging, balancing and flapping whilst reaching for fruit. **Distribution:** Moderately common through eastern coastal forests to Shoalhaven River, NSW with occasional records as far south and west as Wilsons Promontory.

128 ROSE-CROWNED FRUIT-DOVE *Ptilinopus regina* 200–250mm
General: Colourful medium-sized pigeon with a yellow-lined rose-red cap, marbled grey head and neck, yellow to apricot-coloured breast and bright green wings and back. Females duller. **Voice:** Loud, sad, repeated 'coo-coo-coo-coo…' up to 20 times, getting faster and softer. **Flight:** Fast and direct with a whirring of wings. **Food:** Fruit of rainforest trees (especially figs), palms and vines. **Nest:** Flimsy, see-through assembly of twigs and vine tendrils in dense rainforest areas 2–15m above ground level. 1 pale cream egg. Oct–Feb. **Behaviour:** Forage in canopy, climbing after fruit, hanging upside-down, displaying on bare branches. Often with other fruit-eaters. Presence often revealed by falling fruit. **Distribution:** Coastal N and E Aust. Moderately common to as far south as central Hunter region, but accidental further south with odd records for Vic and Tas.

Birds of the dry country

129 GREY-CROWNED BABBLER *Pomatostomus temporalis* 280–290 mm
General: Dark brown above, warmer brown below, light grey crown, broad white terminal tail-band. **Voice:** Chattering, distinctive 'ya-hoo-ya-hoo'. **Flight:** Low, fast, direct with long glides. **Food:** Insects collected from ground. **Nest:** Dome-shaped, side entrance, in fork of tree or bush. 3–6 pale or purplish-brown eggs, finely lined brown, Jul–Oct. **Behaviour:** Flocks of 8–12 birds, noisily moving through open forest. Feeding, roosting, breeding as a community. **Distribution:** Seriously declining populations in SE Aust.

130 SUPERB PARROT *Polytelis swainsonii* 360–420 mm
General: Long tailed medium-large green parrot with darker wings and tail. Crown and throat yellow; red chest-band. Female and immature lack chest-band. **Voice:** Prolonged warble, abruptly terminated. **Flight:** Rapid, strong, direct—'effortless'—often quite high. **Food:** Nectar, leaf buds, fruit, seeds (including grasses, eucalypts, acacias). **Nest:** Hole in tree or hollow limb, usually near water and at considerable height. 4–6 white eggs. Spring. **Behaviour:** Timid. Usually singly (adult males), or in pairs or small flocks feeding on the ground or in foliage; nomadic, at least on edge of range. **Distribution:** Moderately common along valleys of Castlereagh and central Murray-Murrumbidgee River systems in NSW; very rare and spasmodic in adjacent areas of Vic (Barmah-Cobram).

131 TURQUOISE PARROT *Neophema pulchella* 190–210 mm
General: Medium-small, green, turquoise blue face, throat and wing; yellow underparts and outer tail-feathers. Male red shoulder patch. Female and immature duller. **Voice:** Feeble, twittering while feeding; also 2-tone whistle. **Flight:** Fluttering erratic flight to nearby tree if disturbed. **Food:** Seeds of grasses and herbaceous plants; orchard fruit. **Nest:** Hole in tree, log or fence-post. 4–5 white eggs. Aug–Dec. **Behaviour:** Usually in pairs or small groups often in open rocky woodlands and forests. Sedentary, some limited seasonal movement. **Distribution:** Rather rare in central NSW and S Qld; rare in parts of NE Vic. Numbers fluctuate. Once considered extinct in Vic, but population apparently increasing.

132 SCARLET-CHESTED PARROT *Neophema splendida* 175–220 mm
General: Medium-small, greenish, blue head, nape and wing-patch, red breast, yellow underparts and outer tail-feathers. Eye dark brown; beak and legs dark greyish. Female and immature duller, lack scarlet chest. **Voice:** Soft musical twitter 'zitt-zitt'. **Flight:** Rapid, direct; just over or through tree tops; erratic flutter when feeding. **Food:** Seeds of grasses and low herbaceous plants; walk along ground feeding, using feet to hold down seed heads of plants. **Nest:** Hole in tree or shrub. 4 white eggs. Spring. **Behaviour:** Unobtrusive, confiding. Usually in pairs, large flocks appear during spasmodic irruptions. Nomadic, sedentary at times, usually seen feeding on ground in grassland savanna mallee or along watercourses. In waterless areas birds apparently obtain moisture from succulents (eg, Calandrinia), or by drinking dew. **Distribution:** Very rare throughout interior of S continental Aust.

133 SCALY-BREASTED LORIKEET
Trichoglossus chlorolepidotus 220–240 mm
General: Medium-sized, all green, distinctive scaly pattern on breast and abdomen; red bill, eyes and underwings. **Voice:** High-pitched screeching and chattering. **Behaviour:** Nomadic. Singly or in small flocks with other lorikeets. Active and noisy, clambering and hanging from flower clumps in eucalypt foliage. Flight swift and direct. Nesting in NSW Aug–Jan; in hollow or knot-hole high in eucalypt, usually 2 round white eggs. **Distribution:** Moderately common around Sydney, rare in south. Aviary escapee populating areas around Melbourne and on Mornington Peninsula.

133

DRY COUNTRY

134 · LITTLE CORELLA *Cacatua sanguinea* 350–390 mm
General: Medium-large short-crested white cockatoo. Short bill white, pink feathering in front of eye and dark blue eye-ring. Underparts tinged yellow. **Voice:** Loud wavering high-pitched shriek. **Flight:** Slow, deliberate, few wing-beats then a glide like Galahs. **Food:** Bulbs, seeds, roots and herbage of various plants. **Nest:** Hole in tree, also sometimes in cliff cavities and ant nests. 3 white eggs. Spring. **Behaviour:** Usually in noisy flocks; in other parts of Aust flocks of up to 32,000 birds have been recorded, in the SE usually much smaller. Ground-feeder, preferring savanna and red gum areas. **Distribution:** Rare in NW Vic; abundant throughout dry interior of Aust.

135 · LONG-BILLED CORELLA *Cacatua tenuirostris* 380–410 mm
General: Medium-large white cockatoo with long curved pale grey bill, red forehead and traces of pink to red on the upper breast; bare pale blue skin around eye; short crest usually kept down. Yellowish wash to underparts, obvious in flight. **Voice:** Screeching and quavering 'kurrup' call. **Food:** Digs for roots, bulbs and corms, especially of introduced onion grass, and sprouting cereal crops. **Flight:** Fast and direct with quick shallow wing-beats. **Nest:** On rotting sticks and leaves placed in tree hollow. 2–3 white eggs; Jul–Nov. **Behaviour:** Local populations may roost and feed in large cohesive flocks. May circle many times before roosting or before finally leaving roosting site in the morning, calling loudly. **Distribution:** Favours River Red Gum country. Once widespread in inland SE Aust. Range diminished, but locally common in W Vic and E SA with flocks increasing along E coastal areas between Brisbane and Moulamein, NSW. Small population in E Tas.

136 · MAJOR MITCHELL'S COCKATOO *Cacatua leadbeateri* 350–400 mm
General: Medium-large white and pink parrot with red, yellow and white banded crest. Male has brown, female pale reddish iris. **Voice:** Screeching and peculiar plaintive quavering cry 'creeek-eery-creee'. **Flight:** Distinctive shallow and irregular wing-beats interspersed with short glides. **Food:** Omnivorous. Seeds of grasses and herbs, fruits, roots, bulbs, leaves and insect larvae. **Nest:** In hollow or broken-off stump; lined with decaying debris, bark strips and leaves. 2–4 white eggs. Aug–Dec. **Behaviour:** Singly, in pairs or small nomadic flocks in arid eucalypt, pine or Black Box open forests. Very shy. Reported to favour 'camel or pie melons'. **Distribution:** Once widespread and moderately common through arid inland but numbers are declining in NW Vic; and arid areas of SA. It is now considered vulnerable in W NSW.

DRY COUNTRY

HONEYEATERS CHARACTERISTICS

These honeyeaters are rarely seen on the S and E slopes of the Great Divide. The Grey-fronted Honeyeater is sedentary in some localities but, usually nomadic, moving either singly or in small groups through the canopy and lower levels of the bush in search of nectar, berries and insects. The presence of most honeyeaters usually first indicated by loud, sweet, persistent calls, often uttered as the bird flies to a considerable height before rapidly dropping to the treetops. The Pied Honeyeater, with its 'tetice-tee-tee' call (similar to that of the Little Grassbird) frequently does this, contrasting with the monotonous whistle of the Black and the 'georgie-georgie-georgie' song of the Painted Honeyeater. The nests of honeyeaters are usually cup-shaped, of grass and twigs lined with softer material. Usually 2 pale eggs, blotched with darker tones, are laid.

137 PAINTED HONEYEATER *Grantiella picta* 150–170 mm
General: Medium-small brownish-black bird with white underparts and yellow flash on wing. Female is smaller and is less brown. **Behaviour:** Migrant, usually in small flocks, feeding on mistletoe berries and nectar which appear to be its staple diet. **Distribution:** Rather rare throughout inland E Aust, a summer visitor to ironbark and similar forests.

138 BLACK HONEYEATER *Certhionyx niger* 100–130 mm
General: Small dark bird with white underparts and blackish breast. Female brownish with white eyebrow. **Behaviour:** Nomadic in small flocks in arid mallee scrub and woodland. Female builds nest; both birds hatch and feed young. **Distribution:** Moderately common throughout arid S Aust. Rare in Vic.

139 PIED HONEYEATER *Certhionyx variegatus* 150–180 mm
General: Medium-small black bird with white abdomen and wing-patch. Female and immature birds are brownish grey with whitish wing marks and abdomen. **Behaviour:** In migratory or nomadic flocks or pairs in arid heath and woodland. **Distribution:** Common in arid interior of continent. Very rare in SE Aust.

SIMILAR SPECIES

Brown-headed Honeyeater 110–140mm (2:28)

Fuscous Honeyeater 150–160mm (7:84)

140 BLACK-CHINNED HONEYEATER *Melithreptus gularis* 160–170mm
General: Medium-small, greenish-yellow, white underparts, black throat-stripe. Head black, white bands behind eye and on nape, bluish eyebrow crescent. **Nest:** Fragile bark and grass cup high in canopy, 2 pinkish eggs, orange spotted. Jul–Dec. **Behaviour:** Usually small nomadic flocks with other honeyeaters searching foliage for large insects, spiders. **Distribution:** Rather rare in SE Aust drier woodlands, more common in north. **Similar species:** White-naped Honeyeater 130–150mm (2:28).

141 GREY-FRONTED HONEYEATER *Lichenostomus plumulus* 130–160mm
General: Small, resembles Yellow-plumed Honeyeater but with less conspicuous breast streaking and dark upper edge to yellow ear tuft. **Voice:** Shrill canary-like song; 'wirt-wirt-wirt-wirt' flight call; repeated 'clit' contact call. **Food:** Nectar, seeds, fruit and insects; usually in mallee eucalypts or mistletoes. **Nest:** Deep cup of grass, plant fibres, spider web and bark strips; lined with feathers, fur or down; 2 pink eggs with small chestnut flecks; Sept–Dec in south. **Behaviour:** In pairs in taller trees of arid woodlands, sometimes mallee and scrub. Very similar in habits to White-plumed Honeyeater (2:28). **Distribution:** Common in arid NSW and interior of Aust. Very rare in south-east. **Similar species:** Yellow-plumed Honeyeater 130–160mm (5:56).

142 WHITE-CHEEKED HONEYEATER *Phylidonyris nigra* 160–180mm
General: Like New Holland Honeyeater, but brown eye and larger white cheek patch and no white tips to outer tail-feathers. **Behaviour:** Active and noisy feeder on nectar and insects; swift and erratic flight. Call a melodious warbling 'twee-ee, twee-ee', 'ee-chip' and 'tu-tu'. Rough cup nest of twigs, grass and bark in low shrub; 2 yellow-buff eggs, spotted brown; Aug–Dec. **Distribution:** Coastal E Aust, usually in heathland. Moderately common to as far south as Jervis Bay. Vagrant to Vic. **Similar species:** New Holland Honeyeater 170–180mm (2:82).

SIMILAR SPECIES

White-naped Honeyeater
130–150mm (2:28)

Yellow-plumed Honeyeater
130–160mm (5:56)

New Holland Honeyeater
170–180mm (2:82)

143 GROUND CUCKOO-SHRIKE *Coracina maxima* 330–360 mm

General: Medium-large, light-grey, darker face and black wings; underparts lighter. Black bars on lower back, upper tail and abdomen. Black tail forked with white tips on outer feathers. Eye pale yellow; beak, legs blackish. **Voice:** Rippling call, usually uttered in flight, 'kee-lick, kee-lick, kee-lick' or 'cheer-er cheer-er'. **Flight:** Direct, undulating. **Food:** Insects and other small creatures, foraged on ground. **Nest:** Small, shallow cup (60–70 mm diameter); of grasses, twigs and wool bound with cobwebs; usually on horizontal fork well above ground. 2–3 greenish eggs; heavily marked with brown, usually on larger end. Aug–Nov. Two females sometimes lay eggs in same nest. **Behaviour:** Nomadic, in pairs or small flocks; usually feeding or running rapidly on ground; moving head back and forth like pigeon. If disturbed flies to nearby tree. **Distribution:** Very rare to rather rare throughout arid Aust. Occasionally seen in vicinity of Murray R in N Vic.

144 SPOTTED BOWERBIRD *Chlamydera maculata* 250–300 mm

General: Medium-sized, brown; darker back and wings heavily spotted buff. Underparts lighter; brown mottling on breast and barring on flanks. Opalescent lilac plumes on nape, white terminal tail-band. Female similar; but smaller, less prominent plumes. Eye brown, beak black, legs olive-green. **Voice:** Harsh cat-like cry; also excellent mimic of other birds. **Flight:** Direct, fast, undulating. **Food:** Omnivorous. Berries, fruits, seeds and insects, usually from foliage. Often seen in native fig in arid Aust. Very fond of orchard fruit. **Nest:** Saucer-shaped of twigs, lined with grasses; usually in canopy of leafy tree or shrub. 2 pale yellowish-green eggs covered haphazardly with purple lines. Oct–Dec. **Behaviour:** In pairs during breeding; in small flocks at other times. Constructs bower of thick parallel lines of interwoven sticks and grass, about 60 cm in length and 25 cm high; under tree or bush and decorated with bones, shells and bright objects, particularly silver ones. Sticks often 'painted' with crushed vegetable material. **Distribution:** Rare throughout interior of E Aust. Sometimes occurs along Murray R in NW Vic, as far east as Swan Hill.

SIMILAR SPECIES		ASSOCIATED WILDLIFE

White-bellied Cuckoo-shrike 260–280 mm (7:68)	Black-faced Cuckoo-shrike 300–360 mm (2:16)	Red Gum

145 WHITE-BROWED TREECREEPER *Climacteris affinis* 140–150mm

General: Small, brown, white eyebrow. Head and neck darker brown; throat and breast grey; sharply defined from striated abdomen. Black sub-terminal tail-band; orange wing-stripe. Eye dark brown; beak and legs black. Female chestnut on throat and above eyebrow. **Voice:** Includes sharp, staccato call like White-throated Treecreeper; also soft piping. **Flight:** Short, undulating, from canopy of tree to base of another tree. **Food:** Insects and their larvae from under bark, or on ground. **Nest:** Usually in hollow limb; lined with grasses, down and fur. 3 pinkish eggs, spotted with darker reddish tones. Aug–Nov. **Behaviour:** Singly or in pairs, moving quietly through mallee and woodland particularly pine and belar stands in Vic. Spirals up tree in search of food; feeds extensively on ants found on ground near bases of trees. **Distribution:** Rare throughout arid interior of continent. In Vic confined to north-west; in NSW confined to west.

146 BLACK-FACED WOODSWALLOW *Artamus cinereus* 175–200mm

General: Medium-small, dark, smoke-grey, lighter underparts. Black face and outer tail-feathers tipped white. Eye brown; legs and beak grey with black tip on beak. Juvenile mottled grey. **Voice:** Twittering 'quet-quet'; usually uttered in flight. **Food:** Insects, caught in flight or taken on ground. **Nest:** Saucer-shaped; of grasses and roots placed low in tree or shrub or even inside sheds. 3–4 glossy white eggs, blotched brown and purple. Aug–Dec. **Behaviour:** Usually in fairly sedentary small flocks, often with other Woodswallows, particularly White-browed Woodswallows. Loose flocks of Woodswallows perch on trees, telegraph lines and use these vantage points to gather food in the air, or alight on ground to forage. **Distribution:** Common in woodland savanna of interior Aust. Only occasionally seen in coastal regions of SE Aust, except during droughts.

SIMILAR SPECIES ASSOCIATED WILDLIFE

Brown Treecreeper 160–180mm (5:42)

Masked Woodswallow 175–190mm (5:34)

Dusky Woodswallow 170–180mm (2:18)

Scrubby Cypress-pine

147 SPECKLED WARBLER *Chthonicola sagittata* 115–125mm
General: Small, brownish, ground-frequenting. **Voice:** Sweet song with some mimicry; scolding notes. **Food:** Insects, some seeds collected on ground. **Nest:** Grass and bark domed nest lined with fur. 3–4 dark red-brown eggs. Aug–Jan. **Behaviour:** Gregarious, often in flocks with other species. Confiding. Flight interspersed with hopping. Good mimic. Parasitised by Black-eared Cuckoo (5:58). **Distribution:** Moderately common, becoming rarer. Sedentary in drier open woodlands of SE mainland ranges, especially where undergrowth is sparse.

148 WHITE-BREASTED WOODSWALLOW *Artamus leucorhynchus* 160–180mm
General: Medium-small, dark grey-brown upperparts, head with neat demarcation from white chest and abdomen. White rump, all dark tail. Other woodswallows have white-tipped tail. **Voice:** 'Pert-pert' call, pleasant song, sometimes with mimicry. **Flight:** Graceful, wheeling, drifting—darting after insects from tree perch. **Food:** Insects, often caught over water. **Nest:** Nest of cups and twigs high in tree, or in old nest of other birds; often over water. 3–4 pale pink eggs freckled brown. Aug–Jan. **Behaviour:** Nomadic. Pairs or small flocks. Many migrate to SE for nesting. **Distribution:** N and E Aust, S to N Vic. **Similar species:** White-browed Woodswallow 180–210mm (5:34).

149 HOODED ROBIN *Melanodryas cucullata* 140–170mm
General: Male upperparts and throat black, breast and wing-bars white. Female grey and white instead of black and white. **Voice:** Feeble, high-pitched descending trill; often calls at night and at dawn. High chatter when alarmed. **Flight:** Short, undulating; not fast. **Food:** Insects and spiders, usually collected on ground. **Nest:** Cup-shaped; of grasses and strips of bark bound with cobwebs and lined with fine material, in low fork. 2 blue-green eggs tinted brown on larger end. Spring. **Behaviour:** Usually in nomadic pairs in eucalypt, cypress-pine and wattle savanna, searching among fallen timber. If disturbed near nest feigns injury to lead intruder away. **Distribution:** Moderately common SE inland, but distribution shrinking in south.

SIMILAR SPECIES

Striated Grasswren
145–195mm (5:26)

Shy Heathwren
115–140mm (5:28)

White-browed Woodswallow
180–210mm (5:34)

DRY COUNTRY

150 WESTERN GERYGONE *Gerygone fusca* 100–110mm
General: Very small, pale grey-brown, lighter underparts and white base of ash-brown tail. Eyebrow pale grey, eye red-brown; beak, legs black. **Voice:** Sweet, pensive varied; prolonged 'up and down the scale'; similar to White-throated Gerygone. **Flight:** Short, weak, fluttering flight from tree to tree. **Food:** Scale and other insects found in leaves. **Nest:** Oval, with hooded side entrance; of fine fibres and web, lined with feathers; hung in outer foliage. 2–3 pinkish eggs, speckled red on larger end. **Behaviour:** Usually in pairs; friendly; in canopy of open forests and scrub. **Distribution:** Migratory. Rather rare in SE Aust, more common in the arid woodlands, further inland.

151 WESTERN (Mallee) WHIPBIRD *Psophodes nigrogularis leucogaster* 200–260mm
General: Medium-sized, crested, olive upperparts, light grey underparts; dark brown on flight feathers. **Voice:** Lacks 'whip-crack' of Eastern Whipbird. Ventriloquial; harsh, distinctive series of rattling notes, usually in early morning or evening, possibly a duet. Increases in volume as call proceeds. **Flight:** Short, rapid, feeble, prefers to run. **Food:** Insects and their larvae found on ground. **Nest:** Fairly large, shallow bowl; of very fine vegetable material, low to ground in bush. 2 pale blue eggs marked brown and black. Jul–Oct. **Behaviour:** Very shy, usually in pairs or small groups moving rapidly through mallee scrub, often with tail erect, or hopping among litter in search of food. **Distribution:** Very rare in Big Desert areas of NW Vic and adjacent SA. Critically endangered. See discussion on Western Whipbird (5:12).

152 CHIRRUPING WEDGEBILL *Psophodes cristatus* 190–210mm
General: Medium-small, brown, crested, wing-feathers tipped white. Tail often outspread, and white marks conspicuous. **Voice:** Sweet, sad and penetrating; 'Sweet Kitty Lintock' or 'Did you get drunk'; usually from top of bush; increases in volume as song continues. **Flight:** Rapid, close to ground with tail fanned. **Food:** Insects and larvae from ground litter, occasionally seeds. **Nest:** Loose, flattened cup-shape of twigs; low to ground in low bushes or saltbush. 2–3 blue-green eggs with few black spots. Spring. **Behaviour:** In pairs or small flocks, often associated with Babblers, hopping, through low scrub and saltbush along watercourses. **Distribution:** Common in arid central Aust but extremely rare in SE Aust. Still sighted in W NSW.

SIMILAR SPECIES

White-throated Gerygone
100–115mm (2:14)

Yellow Thornbill
85–100mm (2:12)

Weebill 80–90mm (5:54)

153. AUSTRALIAN PRATINCOLE *Stiltia isabella* 220–240 mm
General: Medium-sized, long-legged, brownish, ground-frequenting, long black-tipped wings. Throat grey, white rump conspicuous in flight. Short square tail black with white outer feathers. Eye and legs brown, black bill red at base. **Voice:** Pleasant whistle or 'tu-whee'. **Flight:** Rapid, 'tern-like'; sudden changes of direction. **Food:** Insects and their larvae, collected on ground and in air. **Nest:** Depression or clear space on ground. 2 sand-coloured eggs, blotched darker. Sept–Feb. **Behaviour:** Usually in flocks, feeding on arid plains, hawking for insects or drinking at dams and tanks. Well camouflaged on ground, edges of roads, claypans and landing strips. Mixed flocks with Inland Dotterel and sometimes Oriental Pratincole. **Distribution:** Common throughout arid central and coastal Aust. Both sedentary and nomadic in N areas, some north-south migration. Rather rare summer migrant to drier areas of SE Aust. Resembles Oriental Pratincole (230–240 mm), a rare migrant to SE Aust, occasional stragglers occur in the south.

154. INLAND (Australian) DOTTEREL *Charadrius australis* 190–200 mm
General: Medium-small, ground-frequenting, mottled brown above, face and underparts whitish with prominent black 'Y' on breast, vertical black band on head. **Voice:** Metallic 'quack'. **Flight:** Rapid, strong. Reluctant to fly preferring to run or sit depending on camouflage for protection. **Food:** Insects and seeds, collected from ground. **Nest:** 3 buff eggs, strongly blotched with brown, especially on larger end, laid on ground. When nest unattended eggs covered with litter or pellets of dry earth. Birds perform 'broken wing' act to distract intruders from nest site. **Behaviour:** Usually pairs or flocks, nomadic in north of range and migratory in south. When feeding bobs head. Usually near water on arid scrub areas, inland and coastal plains. Often seen in mixed flocks with Pratincoles. **Distribution:** Moderately common in central and S inland; rare summer migrant to SE.

SIMILAR SPECIES

Oriental Pratincole (p.34)

Black-fronted Dotterel
160–180 mm (4:76)

Red-kneed Dotterel
170–190 mm (4:76)

HAWK CHARACTERISTICS

Medium-large to very large predators with hooked beaks, large eyes and talons. Nest in higher limbs of tall trees, building large rough platform nests lined with leaves; often rebuilding their own or other birds' old abandoned nests. Eggs are generally light stone colour, spotted with darker shades. Of those illustrated all except the Collared Sparrowhawk are inland species. All eat small insects, reptiles, marsupials and rodents, but the Collared Sparrowhawk and Grey Falcon also include birds in their diets.

155 BLACK-BREASTED BUZZARD *Hamirostra melanosternon* 510–610mm
General: Large, dark or light, brown collar, shoulder, mantle and underparts. Short grey square tail. White 'bulls-eye' on wing distinct in flight. 2 phases: one mainly black, other light rufous-brown. **Behaviour:** Singly or in pairs, soaring at considerable heights over arid open country and woodlands in search of lizards, rabbits, etc. Call similar to Whistling Eagle's; short and piercing. Rare, occasionally seen in SE Aust.

156 GREY FALCON *Falco hypoleucos* 300–440mm
General: Medium-large, blue-grey, very pale underparts, darker wing-tips. Immature darker, with dark grey head. **Behaviour:** Usually singly or pairs; leisurely circling or diving very rapidly after prey in arid woodlands. Call a loud repeated 'cuck-cuck'. Rare in SE Aust.

157 LETTER-WINGED KITE *Elanus scriptus* 350–425mm
General: Medium-large, light grey, black 'shoulders' on upperwing and black 'W' on underwings. Pale underparts. Male call 'kack, kack, kack'; female 'kar, kar, kar'. **Behaviour:** Singly, pairs, sometimes flocks. Hovers expertly, legs lowered, tail depressed, searching for prey in savanna grasslands of Aust interior; occasionally seen in SE with locust and mouse plagues.

158 COLLARED SPARROWHAWK *Accipiter cirrhocephalus* 300–400mm
General: Medium-large, dark grey upperparts, rufous collar and rufous underparts, finely barred white. Middle toe very long. Immature browner, with coarser barring. **Behaviour:** Singly or pairs, flying rapidly close to ground in search of prey. Shrill shattering call; flies rapidly through branches in search of smaller birds. Rather rare, throughout Aust, Tas and New Guinea.

SIMILAR SPECIES

Brown Goshawk 400–500mm (2:46)   Black-shouldered Kite 330–380mm (7:30)

Birds of the northern plains

NORTHERN SPECIES

Many rare species and sub-species have already been described in other books, especially *Birds 5: Dry Country*, in this series. Rather than duplicate the descriptions, these birds are only illustrated here and a page reference given to the appropriate book for further information.

159 Little Corella 350–390mm (p92) **160** Pied Butcherbird 320–360mm (5:72) **161** Black-eared Cuckoo 190–210mm (5:58) **162** Redthroat 90–115mm (5:18) **163** Chestnut-crowned Babbler 210–230mm (5:48) **164** Mallee Emu-wren 130–150mm (5:26) **165** Red-lored Whistler 190–220mm (5:32) **166** Striated Grasswren 145–195mm (5:26) **167** Rufous Fieldwren 115–135mm (5:16) **168** Chestnut Quail-thrush 200–260mm (5:46) **169** Black-eared Miner 230–260mm (5:40) **170** Spotted Nightjar 290–330mm (5:62) **171** Apostlebird 290–330mm (5:66) **172** Malleefowl 550–610mm (5:44) **173** Plumed Whistling-Duck 400–620mm (p60)

NORTHERN PLAINS

Bird list and index

All rare, very rare, accidental and vagrant birds recorded in south-eastern Australia, until July 2003, are listed here. References to look-alike birds are also provided.

The first column lists the **common name** of rare birds. Those featured in this book are shown in bold.

The second column indicates the **page number**, for this book shown in bold. Page references are usually to the text, and generally a bird described in the text is illustrated on the facing page. Occasionally a page reference may be to a small illustration only. If a bird is more fully described in another book in this series then a cross-reference (book and page number, eg, 3:54) to that description is provided. An asterisk (★) indicates that a bird is not illustrated in this series.

The third column indicates the **present status** of the bird in its preferred habitat within the region. Frequency is shown in seven groups: very common (VC); common (C); moderately common (MC); rather rare (RR); rare (R); very rare (VR); or not yet recorded from the region but recorded nearby (NR).

The fourth column summarises its **preferred habitat**.

The fifth column indicates the **worldwide range** of the species.

The sixth and last column describes **occurrence**—whether a bird is sedentary (S), nomadic (N) or migratory (M). An asterisk (*) in this column indicates that the bird has been recorded as a breeding species for the region.

All the birds described and illustrated in this seven-book series are listed in the complete index in *Birds 1: Urban Areas*.

COMMON BIRD NAME	PAGE	Regional status	Habitat	Range	OCCUR
Albatross, Black-browed	3:12	C	Oceans, bays	S oceans	M
Grey-headed	**16**	R–RR	Open oceans	S oceans	M
Light-mantled Sooty	**16**	VR	Open oceans	Sub-Antarctic oceans	M
Royal	**16**	VR	Open oceans	S oceans	M
Shy	3:12	MC	Oceans, bays	Aust, NZ oceans	M
Sooty	**16**	VR	Open oceans	S oceans	M
Wandering	3:12	MC	Open oceans	S oceans	M
Yellow-nosed	**16**	R	Open oceans	S oceans	M
Apostlebird	**111** 5:66	R	Arid open forest	Central E Aust	S*
Babbler, Chestnut-crowned	**110** 5:48	R	Mallee, open forests	Interior, SE Aust	S/N*
Grey-crowned	**88**	RR–R	Open forests	E Aust	S*
White-browed	**12**	MC	Savanna, scrubs	Interior	S*
Bittern, Black	★	VR	Wetlands	N, E &SW Aust	S
Little	**62**	VR	Wetlands	Coastal E & S Aust, Africa, W Eurasia	S*
Black-Cockatoo, Glossy	**66**	VR	Dense forests	Coastal E Aust	S*
Red-tailed	**66**	R–RR	Savanna, forests	All states, not Tas	S*
Yellow-tailed	**66** 2:42	MC	Woodland	SE Aust	N
Booby, Brown	**24**	R–VR	Coastal	All tropical waters	M
Bowerbird, Regent	**68**	RR	Rainforest margins	E Aust	S

COMMON BIRD NAME	PAGE	Regional status	Habitat	Range	OCCUR
Bowerbird, Spotted	98	R	Arid open forests	Interior E Aust	S*
Bristlebird, Eastern	54	VR	Coastal scrub	E Aust	S*
Rufous	54	VR	Coastal heaths	W Vic, E SA	S*
Brolga	3 4:32	R	Grasslands, swamps	N & E Aust	S/N
Bustard, Australian	48	VR	Savanna	Aust, PNG	S/N*
Butcherbird, Pied	110 5:72	RR	Woodland	Aust, not south	S*
Button-quail, Little	52 7:36	MC	Grasslands	Aust mainland	N
Red-backed	50	VR	Grasslands, swamps	Coastal NE & SE Aust	N*
Red-chested	52	R	Grasslands	E Aust	N*
Buzzard, Black-breasted	108	VR	Savanna	Interior Aust	N*
Catbird, Green	68	R	Rainforests	Coastal E Aust	S
Cicadabird	74	R	Dense forest	Coastal E & N Aust, NG & adjacent islands	M*
Cockatoo (see also Black-Cockatoo; Corella)					
Major Mitchell's	92	RR	Open woodland	Interior Aust	N
Corella, Little	92, 110	R	Savanna, scrubs	N Central Aust	N*
Long-billed	92	RR	Savanna	W Vic, E SA	S*
Coucal, Pheasant	80	VR	Coastal heaths, etc	N Aust, NG	S
Crake, Australian Spotted	62 4:60	MC	Wetlands	E & W Aust	N
Baillon's	62 4:60	MC	Wetlands	Aust	M/N
Spotless	62	RR	Coastal wetlands	Aust, NG, SW Pacific Islands	S*
Cuckoo (see also Coucal; Koel)					
Black-eared	110 5:58	R	Open forests, scrubs	Interior Aust, PNG, Indonesia	M
Brush	78	RR	Rainforests, coastal scrubs	N & interior Aust, PNG, Indonesia	S/M*
Channel-billed	80	VR	Woodlands, forests	SE Asia, N & E Aust, PNG	N M* M
Fan-tailed	2:16	VC	All	S & E Aust, Pacific Islands	M
Oriental	80	VR	Rainforests, woodlands	SW Pacific	M
Pallid	5:58	C	All	Aust, Timor, PNG	M
Cuckoo-Dove, Brown	★	VR	Rainforests	E Aust	S
Cuckoo-shrike, Black-faced	74, 98 2:16	C	All	Aust, PNG, Indonesia	M/S
Ground	98	R	Open forests	E Aust, Asia	N
White-bellied	98 7:68	RR–R	Open forests	N & E Aust, PNG, Indonesia	S/M/N
Curlew (see also Stone-curlew)					
Little	36	R	Coastal margins	W Pacific region	M
Dotterel (see also Plover)					
Black-fronted	106 4:76	C	Inland waters	Aust, NZ	S*
Inland	3, 106	R	Arid savanna	Interior Aust	N
Red-kneed	106 4:76	MC	Wetlands	Aust, NZ, PNG	N
Dove (see also Fruit-Dove; Pigeon)					
Bar-shouldered	★	RR	Tropical scrubs	N & E Aust	S
Emerald	86	VR	Rainforests	N & E Aust, SE Asia	S

COMMON BIRD NAME	PAGE	Regional status	Habitat	Range	OCCU
Dowitcher, Asian	**36**	VR	Coastal margins	E Asia	M
Drongo, Spangled	**74**	R	Rainforests	E Aust, NG	M*
Duck (*see also* Whistling-Duck)					
Freckled	**60**	R	Wetlands	S Aust, occ N Aust	N
Dunlin	**32**	VR	Mudflats	N hemisphere	M
Eagle (*see* Kite)					
Egret, Cattle	4:50	MC	Wetlands	Aust, SE Asia	N
Eastern Reef	**40**	R	Coastal margins	Aust, SE Asia, NZ	S
Intermediate	**40**	MC	Wetlands	Aust, Africa, SE Asia	N/M
Emu-wren, Mallee	**110** 5:26	R	Arid heaths, spinifex	NE Vic, SA	S*
Southern	**12** 7:70	RR	Coastal heaths	SE & S Aust	S
Falcon, Grey	**108**	R	Open forests	Interior Aust	N*
Fieldwren, Rufous	**110** 5:16	RR	Heaths	Interior Aust	S*
Figbird, Australasian	**68**	R	Rainforests, mangroves	N & E Aust	N
Finch (*see also* Firetail)					
Double-barred	**56**	RR	Grasslands	N & E Aust	N
Plum-headed	**56**	VR	Tall grasslands	E Aust	M
Spice (*see* Mannikin, Nutmeg)					
Firetail, Beautiful	**56**	R	Coastal scrubs	SE Aust, Tas	S*
Diamond	**12** 7:40	RR	Open woodlands	SE Aust	S
Flycatcher, Leaden	**64** 2:74	MC	Woodlands	N & E Aust	M
Satin	**64** 2:74	MC	Dense forests	E Aust	M
Frigatebird, Great	**24**	VR	Open oceans	Tropical oceans	N
Lesser	**24**	VR	Open oceans	Tropical oceans	N
Fruit-Dove, Rose-crowned	**86**	VR	Rainforests	E Aust, Indonesia	S
Fulmar, Southern	**22**	R	Oceans	S oceans	N
Gannet (*see* Booby)					
Gerygone, Brown	**70**	R	Rainforests	E Aust	S*
Western	**70,104**	RR	Open forests	Interior Aust	M*
White-throated	**104** 2:14	MC	Open woodlands	E & N Aust	M
Giant-Petrel, Northern	3:14	RR	Oceans, bays	Sub-polar, S oceans	N
Southern	3:14	RR	Oceans, bays	Sub-polar, S oceans	N
Godwit, Bar-tailed	3:56	MC	Coastal margins	Worldwide	M
Black-tailed	**36**	R	Coastal margins	Worldwide	M
Goose, Cape Barren	**58**	RR	Coastal islands, plains	S Aust, Tas	N*
Magpie	**58**	VR	Wetlands	Aust, NG	N*
Goshawk, Brown	**42,108** 2:46	MC	Open forests	Aust, NG	S*
Grey	**42**	R	Woodlands, forests	Aust, Pacific Islands	N*
Grasswren, Striated	**102,110** 5:26	RR	Arid heaths, Triodia	Interior SE Aust	S*
Gull, Kelp	**26**	RR	Coastal, oceans	S oceans	N*
Pacific	**26**	C	Coastal	S Aust, Tas	S*
Heathwren, Shy	**102** 5:28	RR	Mallee	S Aust	S*
Heron (*see also* Bittern; Egret)					
Nankeen Night	**62** 4:56	C	Wetlands	Aust, SW Pacific	S/N
Striated	**40**	VR	Coastal margins	N Aust, SE Asia	S
Honeyeater, Black	**94**	R	Open forests	Interior Aust	N*
Black-chinned	**96**	RR	Open forests	E & S Aust	S/N*

COMMON BIRD NAME	PAGE	Regional status	Habitat	Range	OCCUR
Honeyeater, Brown	★	RR	Woodlands, scrubs	N, E & W Aust	S
Brown-headed	94 2:28	MC	Open forests	SE Aust	S/N
Fuscous	94 7:84	RR	Woodlands	E Aust	S/N
Grey-fronted	96	VR	Open forests, scrub	Interior Aust	N*
Lewin's	70	RR	Rainforests	E Aust	S*
New Holland	96 2:82	VC	Forests, heaths	SE & SW Aust	S*
Painted	94	RR	Open forests	Interior E Aust	M
Pied	94	VR	Mallee	Interior Aust	S/N*
Regent	6, 76	VR	Ironbark forests	E ranges Aust	S/N
Scarlet	70	R	Dense forests	E Aust	M/S
White-cheeked	96	MC	Coastal heaths	E & SW Aust	S
White-naped	96 2:28	C	Open forests	SE Aust	S/M
Yellow-plumed	96 5:56	MC	Dry woodlands	S Aust	S*
Yellow-tufted (Helmeted form)	76	VR	Gullies	W Gippsland, Vic	S*
Jabiru (see Stork)					
Jaeger, Arctic	26	MC	Oceans, bays	Sub-polar	M
Long-tailed	26	VR	Oceans	Sub-polar	M
Pomarine	26	R	Oceans	Sub-polar	M
King Parrot, Australian (see Parrot, Australian King)					
Kite (see also Buzzard)					
Black-shouldered	108 7:30	C	All	Aust	N
Brahminy	★	RR	Coastal areas	N & E Aust	S
Letter-winged	108	R	Plains, savanna	Interior Aust	N*
Knot, Great	3:64	R	Coastal margins	Aust, E Asia	M
Red	3:54	RR	Coastal margins	Aust, E Asia	M
Koel, Common	68	VR	Rainforests	E & N Aust, Indonesia	M
Lapwing, Banded	38	RR	Grasslands	N & E Aust	S/N
Lark (see Wagtail)					
Logrunner	★	RR	Rainforest	E Aust	S
Lorikeet, Scaly-breasted	90	RR	Woodlands	E Aust	N
Malleefowl	111 5:44	R	Mallee	Arid S Aust	S*
Mannikin, Chestnut-breasted	★	RR	Grasslands	N & E Aust	N
Nutmeg	56	RR	Coastal scrubs	E Aust	N
Miner, Black-eared	111 5:40	VR	Mallee	Arid S Aust	S*
Monarch, Black-faced	64	R	Rainforests	SE Aust, NG	M
Night Heron, Nankeen (see Heron, Nankeen Night)					
Nightjar, Spotted	78, 111 5:62	RR	Mallee, open forests	Interior Aust	N*
White-throated	78	RR	Coastal forests	E Aust, SE Asia	S*
Osprey	42	VR	Coastal	Worldwide	S
Owl, Barn	48, 82 7:60	C	Open woodlands	Aust	N
Grass	48	VR	Savanna	Aust, SE Asia, Africa	S
Masked	82	RR	Dense forests	Aust, SW Pacific Islands	S*
Powerful	82	R	Coastal forests	SE Aust	S*
Sooty	82	VR	Rainforests	E Aust, NG	S*
Pardalote, Forty-spotted	72	VR	Open forest	E Tas	S*

COMMON BIRD NAME	PAGE	Regional status	Habitat	Range	OCCU
Parrot (*see also* Lorikeet; Rosella)					
Australian King	**84**	MC	Rainforests	E Aust	N*
Blue-winged	**46** 2:40	MC	Open woodlands	SE Aust	M
Bourke's	★	VR	Open woodlands	Interior Aust	N
Elegant	**46**	R	Savanna	S Aust	N
Ground	**44**	VR	Coastal heaths	E & S Aust, Tas	S*
Mulga	**44**	RR	Mallee	S Aust	S
Orange-bellied	**46**	VR	Coastal areas	Vic, SA, Tas	M
Rock	**44**	VR	Coastal areas	SA, SW Aust	S/N
Scarlet-chested	**90**	VR	Mallee	Arid S Aust	N/M*
Superb	**6, 88**	VR	River woodlands	Central SE Aust	S*
Turquoise	**90**	VR–RR	Open woodlands	Central SE Aust	S/N*
Penguin, Adelie	**14**	NR	Oceans	Antarctica	M
Chinstrap	**14**	NR	Oceans	S oceans	M
Erect-crested	**14**	VR	Oceans	S NZ, S Aust	M
Fiordland	**14**	RR	Oceans	S NZ, S Aust	M
King	**14**	VR	Oceans	Sub-Antarctic	M
Macaroni (Royal)	**14**	NR	Oceans	Macquarie Island, Aust	M
Rockhopper	**14**	MC–R	Oceans	Sub-Antarctic	M
Snares	**14**	NR	Oceans	S NZ waters	M
Petrel (*see also* Giant-Petrel; Prion; Storm-Petrel)					
Blue	**18**	VR	Oceans	S oceans	M
Gould's	**18**	VR	Oceans	E Aust	M
Great-winged	**18**	R	Oceans	S oceans	M
Grey	**20**	VR	Oceans	Sub-Antarctic	M
Kerguelen	**18**	VR	Oceans	Sub-Antarctic	M
Mottled	**18**	R	Oceans	NZ & Aust waters	M
Soft-plumaged	**18**	R	Oceans	S oceans	M
White-chinned	**20**	VR	Oceans	Sub-Antarctic	M
Phalarope, Red-necked	3:64	VR	Water margins	Worldwide	M
Wilson's	**36**	VR	Water margins	N & S America, Pacific rim	M
Pheasant Coucal (*see* Coucal, Pheasant)					
Pigeon (*see also* Dove; Fruit-Dove)					
Topknot	**86**	A	Rainforests	Coastal E Aust	S
White-headed	★	RR	Rainforest	E Aust	N
Wonga	**84**	RR	Dense forests	E Aust	S*
Plains-wanderer	**52**	R–VR	Grassland	Interior SE Aust	N*
Plover (*see also* Dotterel; Lapwing)					
Greater Sand	**32**	R	Lake & coast margins	Interior Aust	N*
Grey	3:50	R	Coastal margins	Worldwide	M
Hooded	**38**	R	Coastal margins	S Aust	S*
Lesser Sand	**32**	RR	Coastal margins	Asia, Africa, SW Pacific	M
Oriental	**32**	VR	Coastal margins	Asia, Africa, SW Pacific	M
Pratincole, Australian	**3, 106**	RR	Arid plains	Aust, NG	M

COMMON BIRD NAME	PAGE	Regional status	Habitat	Range	OCCUR
Pratincole, Oriental	34, 106	VR	Arid plains	Africa, S Asia, Aust	M
Prion, Broad-billed	22	VR	Oceans	S oceans	M
Fairy	22	MC	Oceans	S oceans	M
Fulmar	★	A	Oceans	Oceans	M
Salvin's	22	RR	Oceans	S oceans	M
Slender-billed	22	RR	Oceans	S oceans	M
Quail (see also Button-quail)					
Californian	★	VR	Grasslands	King Island	S
King	50	VR	Coast swamps, heaths	SE Asia, N & E Aust	S*
Quail-thrush, Chestnut	111 5:46	R	Mallee	Interior S Aust	S*
Redthroat	110 5:18	R	Mallee	Arid S Aust	S*
Robin, Hooded	102	RR	Woodlands, scrubs	Aust mainland	S*
Rosella, Crimson	84 2:42	VC	Dense forests	SE Aust	S/N
Ruff/Reeve	62	VR	Wetlands	Worldwide	M
Sanderling	3:62	MC	Ocean beaches	Worldwide	M
Sandpiper (see Birds 3: Oceans, Bays and Beaches for descriptions of other sandpipers)					
Broad-billed	34	R	Coastal margins	Worldwide	M
Buff-breasted	34	VR	Grasslands, lake edges	N & S America, SE Aust	M
Common	36	RR	Coastal, wetlands	Eurasia, A'asia	M
Marsh	3:64	RR	Coastal, wetlands	Worldwide	M
Pectoral	34	R	Wetlands	Pacific region	M
Terek	34	VR	Coastal margins	E hemisphere	M
White-rumped	34	VR	Wetlands, tidal margins	S Aust	M
Wood	36	RR	Coastal, wetlands	E hemisphere	M
Scrubwren, Large-billed	72	R	Rainforests	E Aust	S*
Sea-Eagle (see Kite)					
Shearwater, Flesh-footed	20	R	Oceans	S Indian & Pacific oceans	M
Hutton's	20	R	Oceans	NZ waters	N
Little	20	VR	Oceans	S oceans	N
Sooty	20	RR	Oceans	S oceans	M
Wedge-tailed	20	R	Oceans	Pacific & Indian Oceans	N
Skua (see also Jaegar)					
Great	26	RR	Oceans	S oceans	M
Snipe, Painted	38	R	Wetlands	Africa, SE Asia, Aust	S/N*
Sparrowhawk, Collared	108	R	Open forests	Aust, Tas, NG	N*
Starling, Common	74 1:26	VC	Urban	SE Aust	S/N*
Stint, Long-toed	32	VR	Coastal, wetlands	E Asia, A'asia	M
Stone-curlew, Beach	★	VR	Beach	N & E Aust	S
Bush	13, 38 5:22	RR	Open forests	Aust	S*
Stork, Black-necked	58	VR	Wetlands	N & E Aust, S Asia	N
Storm-Petrel, Grey-backed	22	NR	Oceans	All oceans	M
Leach's	22	VR	Oceans	N hemisphere	M
Wilson's	22	RR	Oceans	S oceans	M
Swift, Fork-tailed	80	RR	All	Central Asia, Aust	M

COMMON BIRD NAME	PAGE	Regional status	Habitat	Range	OCCU
Tattler, Grey-tailed	3:62	R	Coastal margins	W Pacific region	M
Tern, Antarctic	**30**	VR	Coastal	S oceans	N
Arctic	**30**	VR	Coastal	Worldwide	M
Common	**30**	R	Coastal	Worldwide	M
Fairy	**28**	RR	Coastal	W & S Aust	S/M*
Gull-billed	**30**	RR	Wetlands	Almost worldwide	M*
Little	**28**	RR	Coastal	SE Asia, Aust	M
Roseate	**28**	VR	Coastal	N hemisphere, Aust	M
White-fronted	**30**	RR	Coastal	SW Pacific Ocean	M
White-winged Black	**30**	RR	Coastal, wetlands	Worldwide temp oceans	M
Thornbill, Brown	**70** 1:60	VC	Woodlands	E Aust	S
Buff-rumped	**10** 2:14	RR	Woodlands	E Aust	S
Yellow	**104** 2:12	MC	Woodlands	SE mainland	S
Thrush (*see* Quail-thrush)					
Treecreeper, Brown	**100** 5:42	MC	Dry woodlands	E Aust	S
Red-browed	**72**	RR	Rainforests	E Aust	N*
White-browed	**100**	R	Belar-pine	Interior S Aust	N*
Triller, White-winged	**74** 2:18	MC	Open woodlands	Aust, PNG	N/M
Tropicbird, Red-tailed	**24**	VR	Oceans	Tropical oceans	N
Wagtail, Yellow	★	A	Wetlands	SE Asia	N
Warbler (*see also* Gerygone)					
Speckled	**102**	RR	Dry woodlands	E Aust	S*
Wedgebill, Chirruping	**104**	VR	Saltbush	Interior Aust	S*
Weebill	**104** 5:54	C	Drier woodlands	Aust mainland	S*
Whimbrel	3:56	R	Coastal margins	W Pacific region	M
Whipbird, Western	**104**	VR	Mallee scrub	Interior S Aust	S*
Whistler, Gilbert's	5:32	RR	Drier scrubs	Interior S Aust	S/N
Red-lored	**110** 5:32	R	Mallee	Interior S Aust	S*
Whistling-Duck, Plumed	**60,111**	R	Wetlands	N & E Aust	N
Wandering	**60**	VR	Wetlands	N Aust, Indonesia	N
Whiteface, Southern	**10** 5:20	MC	Dry scrubs	S Aust	S*
Woodswallow, Black-faced	**100**	R	Savanna, open forest	Interior Aust, Timor	M*
Dusky	**100** 2:18	VC	Woodland	E & S Aust	M/S*
Masked	**100** 5:34	MC	Woodland, scrubs	Aust mainland	M
White-breasted	**102**	RR	Woodland near water	N & E Aust	M
White-browed	**102** 5:34	MC	Forest margins	Aust	N
Wren (see Emu-wren; Fieldwren; Grasswren)					

If a bird resembling any of the species illustrated in this book is found dead, it should be deep frozen and then sent or delivered to your local museum or regional wildlife officer. If a dead bird is found with a leg-band or wing-tag, the band or tag should be forwarded to Australian Bird and Bat Banding Scheme, Environment Australia, PO Box 8, Canberra, ACT 2601 with date and locality of the finding.